Power Plays

Decision-Making Power · God-Pleasing Power ·
World-Changing Power

preTeen ELECTIVES AGES 10-12

A Curriculum for Preteens
ages 10-12

STANDARD PUBLISHING
Cincinnati, Ohio

Power Plays

About the Authors

Churches, conventions, and seminars continue to seek *Linda Kondracki Sibley,* founder and executive director of Confident Kids, to train volunteers to minister to the needs of high-stress kids and families. Linda holds a master's degree in Christian education and pastoral care from Bethel Seminary and has fifteen years experience in church-related ministry to children and families. She is the author of the *Guides for Growing a Healthy Family* series published by Fleming H. Revell and a contributing editor for *Christian Parenting Today.*

Dr. Joyce Hardin is currently the Dean of the College of Education at Lubbock Christian University in Lubbock, Texas. She is the author of *Passport to Adventure,* a Bible curriculum that teaches juniors about missions. A second curriculum entitled *Dare to Be Different* uses critical-thinking skills to help preteens learn to make decisions. Dr. Hardin conducts teacher training workshops throughout the nation and also speaks for retreats and conferences.

Carol Goodlet has been writing Bible-based material for elementary and middle school-age children for ten years. She has taught in Sunday school, youth group, church camp, Vacation Bible School, and children's choir. She is currently a children's curriculum and musical writer for Pilot House Publications.

Cover design and illustration by Dennis Jones
Inside illustrations by Dennis Jones
Computer design by Peggy Theile and Andrew Quach

All Scripture quotations, unless otherwise indicated, are taken from the HOLY BIBLE NEW INTERNATIONAL VERSION®, NIV®. Copyright ©1973, 1978, 1984 by International Bible Society. Used by permission of Zondervan Publishing House. All rights reserved.

The Standard Publishing Company, Cincinnati, Ohio. A Division of Standex International Corporation. ©1997 The Standard Publishing Company
All rights reserved. Printed in the United States of America

03 02 01 00 99 98 97 96   5 4 3 2 1
ISBN 0-7847-0645-X

Power Plays

Beyond childhood, heading to the next level, preteens are bombarded with tough decisions. Help them follow through and evaluate their decisions. Equip them to help others base decisions on God's game plan. Explore their place in world missions. Help them learn the secrets to winning in real life!

Unit 1 — Decision-Making Power — 9

Written by Linda Kondracki Sibley to equip kids to assertively follow through and evaluate their decisions.

Session 1	Power Up! *wise/unwise choices*	16
Session 2	Balancing Act *thinking/feeling wise choices*	24
Session 3	Take Charge!	32
Session 4	I Messed Up!	41
Bridge the Gap	Choosing as a Family	49
Go to Extremes	Choosing to Serve	56

Unit 2 — God-Pleasing Power — 61

Written by Dr. Joyce Hardin to encourage kids to influence others to make godly decisions with time, money, work, leadership, and speech.

Session 1	Leader or Follower?	66
Session 2	Needs, Wants, or Stuff?	73
Session 3	Time: A Commodity or a Resource?	78
Session 4	A Word Is Worth How Much?	84
Bridge the Gap	Things I Do . . . Things You Do	89
Go to Extremes	Leaders Become Servants	96

Unit 3 — World-Changing Power — 100

Written by Carol Goodlet to prepare and involve kids in mission work.

Session 1	Mission Possible	103
Session 2	Salt and Light	108
Session 3	Part of the Team	114
Session 4	Go for the Goal!	118
Bridge the Gap	Missions Banquet	123
Go to Extremes	Toy Auction	125

Why "Next Level"?

Upper elementary kids—we'll call them preteens—are reaching, striving, groping toward the next level. They're in transition. They want to be taller, stronger, faster, and smarter—as they catapult on their way to the next level.

In some ways preteens appear already to have arrived at the next level (once termed junior high). Preteens want to wear the right clothes, match hairstyles with athletes or rock stars, and fit in with the peer group no matter what! For many, however, the next level is an elusive goal: manly muscles and feminine curves are controlled by hormones, not purchasing power.

So, too, the limits on thought structure. Many, if not most, fifth and sixth graders lack the ability to think critically, to form logical arguments, or draw general principles from specific examples. Usually, a wide gulf lies between their level of experience and their ability to reflect on the meaning of their experiences.

Preteens are also still resolving the issue: *What can I do well?* rather than tackling the adolescent question: *Who am I?* So when preteens dress and act like their peers, they are striving for self-acceptance—feeling that they are as current as their peers, rather than establishing a personal identity. Erickson's studies show that ten to twelve year olds are less involved with establishing a personal identity than they are with figuring out what they're really good at. This disparity creates difficulties for those using junior high curriculum for preteen classes: What you see (a teenager) is not what you get (concrete-operational thinking and a different life task).

Next Level curriculum is transitional: to help transitional preteens feel comfortable in teen-style learning settings and to equip leaders to teach within the limits of preteen development. Lessons are structured to help you teach preteens effectively in groups. The younger the student, the more discussion guidance must be given to identify appropriate conclusions, and to suggest appropriate actions to be taken.

While many junior high topics are helpful and many elective curriculums look age appropriate, they often do not work with preteens because they were not designed for preteens' limited thought processing and inexperienced discussion skills.

Next Level Preteen Electives! Planned and designed with preteen issues in mind and tailored for the learning capabilities of concrete thinkers! Visually appealing for the video generation. Emotionally satisfying for techno-driven kids.

This curriculum offers bonus opportunities for preteens to **Go to Extremes** serving others. It also strives to build family relationships—**Bridge the Gap**—during fun-filled family sessions.

So, because life is not a game—
pick a topic and recruit some helpers.
Start a group for ten to twelve year olds—
They'll be glad you did!

Next Level Preteen Electives address the importance of instilling values for character development.

You can use **Next Level Preteen Electives** confidently, knowing that they are based on core biblical principles, permeated with Bible teaching, and presented in a way that ten to twelve year olds can understand and enjoy!

How are Next Level units organized?

Get Into the Game

To introduce the session, this section offers activities to grab the students' attention and encourages participation from the entire group.

These lesson steps offer activity choices that may be set up as learning centers or used as options. Depending on the class size, the teacher may divide the class into smaller groups to complete the activity. Each group works on the activity. For this to be effective, the teacher needs ample assistance.

If the class is small, the teacher can customize the session accordingly. Select one or two options to use or have the class work together instead of dividing into small groups.

Step 1

This activity is designed to help students dig deeper into the topic. This section always includes a biblical study.

Step 2

This section offers another way to discover biblical truth.

Step 3

This activity involves the entire class to help students apply what they learned in Steps 1 and 2.

Take It to the Next Level

This final section ends the session by helping students commit the principles they have learned to their own lives. This section answers the question, "So what does this mean to me personally?"

Extra Helps

Each unit introduction includes devotion suggestions for the teacher and/or the students. The devotional ideas correlate with the sessions in that unit.

Reproducible pages are provided for your convenience. Photocopy these pages for your use or for your students' use to enhance each session.

Additional Resources

The following lists of books and music serve as extra resources for each unit. Feel free to use these materials as research for teaching, or as extra activities.

Unit 1—Decision-Making Power

Secrets of the Best Choice by Lois Walfrid Johnson, Navpress
I Always, Always Have Choices by Linda Kondracki, Fleming H. Revell (a division of Baker Book House)
Kids Choices Game published by Rainfall, Inc., Grand Rapids, MI

Unit 2—God-Pleasing Power

Boundaries by Henry Cloud and John Townsend, Zondervan
How to Manage Your Money by Larry Burkett, Moody
"Seize the Day" by Carolyn Arends (Reunion)

Unit 3—World-Changing Power

52 Ways to Teach Missions by Nancy S. Williamson, Rainbow Books
Anybody Can Be Cool . . . But Awesome Takes Practice by Lorraine Peterson, Bethany House Publishers (specifically Chapter 4)
Out of the Saltshaker: Evangelism as a Way of Life by Rebecca Manley Pippert, Intervarsity Press
"Seed to Sow" by Michael W. Smith (Reunion)
"Love One Another" by Michael W. Smith (Reunion)
"Heart to God, Hand to Man" by Geoff Moore and the Distance (Forefront)
"Face the Nation" by 4Him (Benson)
"We Need Jesus" by Petra (Word)

A Ministry of Confident Kids

If the preteens in your group would benefit from more focused help on the issue of decision making, Standard Publishing offers a distinctively Christian support-group curriculum.

Facing My Feelings
Living in My Family
Making Wise Choices
Growing Through Changes

provides help for hurting kids and struggling parents. Written by Linda Kondracki Sibley, the curriculum guide includes support-group session plans for preschool through preteen, plus a parent guide, and information for program administrators—complete with reproducible forms.

FACING MY FEELINGS helps kids and parents understand that:
- All our feelings are OK.
- We can find healthy ways to talk about and deal with our feelings.
- We have a feeling vocabulary and ways to label what we are feeling.
- Our feelings tell us when we need to ask for help.
- Jesus understands us, and His presence with us is our greatest source of help for facing our feelings.

LIVING IN MY FAMILY helps kids and parents understand that:
- Every family is special and unique.
- No perfect families exist.
- Changes in family life disrupt our sense of security but we can adapt.
- Coping skills help us when our family doesn't or can't meet our needs.
- We need to develop basic skills to communicate in our family.
- Belonging to God's family gives us strength and security.

MAKING WISE CHOICES helps kids and parents understand that:
- We always have choices, no matter what the situation.
- We can follow a process to make wise choices.
- God's Spirit with us is our most valuable resource for choosing wisely.
- We can identify wise people who can help us make intelligent choices.

GROWING THROUGH CHANGES helps kids and parents understand that:
- Change is a natural part of God's design for our world.
- We can respond to change in healthy ways.
- Changed circumstances always pass and hurts heal.
- God is a constant friend and guide through every change.

Unit 1

Decision-Making Power

"I had to do it! I didn't have any choice!" How many times have we heard kids say those words? How many times have they gotten into trouble because they actually believed them? Preteens tend to believe they have no choices. Without thinking, they often base their decisions on what the group wants to do, rather than on what they know to be right. This unit will teach preteens a five step process for making and following through with their own decisions, while relying on God's help to do so. Each week they will practice using these steps as they apply them to their everyday lives. They will learn that their power to make wise choices comes from God, who promises to give them wisdom to choose wisely and courage to follow through with the right choices. Finally, they will learn how to evaluate the results of their choices with the goal of accepting and correcting—not covering up—any mistakes made.

Here is the five step process to follow in making wise choices.

1. Stop. Don't choose too quickly, especially if you're angry. You don't want to make a choice based on how you are feeling at the moment.

2. Think. Consider all the choices you have in this situation. Look for as many as possible; you can always find more than you first think! Consider what the Bible says in every situation.

3. Listen. Pay attention to what your feelings tell you, especially if they say the choice you are about to make is wrong. Feeling uncomfortable about your choice is a warning signal you need to heed.

4. Ask. Seek help, if you need it. Sometimes making a wise choice isn't easy. Asking for help is always a wise choice! You can ask parents, other adults, and God to help you find the right choice.

5. Do. Choose the option you believe is right—and do it! Don't forget to ask for any help you need to carry it out.

Session Summaries

Session 1: Power Up!

To begin this unit, preteens will examine the many kinds of decisions they make and explore the difference between wise and unwise choices. They will also learn that their relationship to God is their greatest source of power in decision making, and they will be given an opportunity to connect with that power source by accepting Jesus as Lord and Savior if they have not already done so.

Know the difference between wise and unwise choices and where to find the power to follow through with difficult choices.

Feel empowered to make and follow through with choices by relying on God's Word and power for guidance.

Identify difficult decision-making situations and ask God for His wisdom and power to help them through one such situation this week.

Session 2: Balancing Act

In this session, preteens will discover that making good decisions is a balancing act between *feeling* and *thinking*. They will explore how making choices based on impulsive feelings often leads to unwise choices, but ignoring their feelings can also get them into trouble! They will learn a five step process that will help them use feelings and thinking to guide them to make wise choices.

Know five steps that can help students balance feelings and thoughts when faced with decisions.

Trust their feelings to guide them (when they take time to think about those feelings).

Practice using the five steps by applying them to a specific decision-making situation in their lives.

Session 3: Take Charge!

Follow through is the main emphasis of this session. Preteens will learn the difference between deciding what to do, and doing what they decide—especially when their wise choice feels scary or hard! They will learn how taking risks and asking for help can help them to effectively follow through with their choices.

Know how taking risks and asking for help empowers students to follow through with wise choices that feel difficult or scary.

Feel motivated to take risks and ask for help when acting on choices they know are right.

Make a plan to follow through on at least one difficult choice.

Session 4: I Messed Up!

The final component of powerful decision making is the ability to evaluate choices honestly, particularly when the decision made was not wise. This session will help preteens learn that making mistakes is part of being human. They can admit to and grow from their mistakes instead of hiding them with hurtful or destructive behaviors.

Know that sometimes everyone makes poor choices and learn how to make a wise choice to correct, instead of cover up, mistakes.

Feel forgiveness when they "mess up" and motivation to choose wisely.

Identify past mistakes and choose better ways to handle similar situations in the future.

Bridge the Gap: Making Choices Together

This session will apply the five steps of making wise choices to the family setting. Families will learn they can work together to solve problems, improve the quality of their lives together, and build family cohesion.

Know how to work as a family to make wise choices that strengthen the quality of their lives.

Feel empowered to make wise choices as a family.

Work as a family to make one choice, and sign a family contract to carry it out.

Go to Extremes: Choosing to Serve

This session will help preteens use the skills learned in this unit to choose and carry out a service project. Although preteens are still developmentally self-centered, they are old enough to understand that God asks us to make conscious choices to care for others' needs. This session will guide them to look at God's Word, think about ways they can serve others, choose a project, and follow through with it.

Know that serving others is a conscious choice we make to obey God's Word.

Feel motivated to plan and participate in a project to serve others.

Carry out a service project.

Devotions

To prepare for this unit, read the following Scriptures, noting how they relate to making wise choices in your life.

Session 1—2 Corinthians 5:17. Having a personal relationship with Jesus is the starting point of powerful decision making.

Session 2—James 1:5. God promises to give us wisdom when we face difficult decision-making situations.

Session 3—Romans 8:37. We can conquer any situation when we trust Jesus to help us see it through.

Session 4—Romans 8:28. God can work all things together for good when we honestly face our mistakes and learn from them.

Extra Helps

Power Packs. Each session contains a Power Verse and a Power Point (slogan) to help your preteens remember key points when facing difficult decisions. Each week these will be added to a poster entitled, "Power to Choose." During the last session, kids will make Power Cards. They will take these home to remind them of their power to make wise choices every day.

"Power to Choose" Poster. The poster will be a visual reminder that armed with their power verses and slogans, they can win any decision making situation they face, no matter how difficult it may seem. To make the poster, photocopy page 13 onto a transparency, project it onto a strip of butcher paper or poster boards (the bigger the better), and trace the outline. You might invite some class members to help you create it.

Pattern for "Power to Choose" poster

©1997 by The Standard Publishing Company. Permission is granted to reproduce this page for ministry purposes only—not for resale.

With Jesus in my heart
to lead the way,
I can make wise choices
everyday!

When my head and my
heart agree,
I've found the choice
that's best for me!

When the choice I've made feels hard—but it's right, asking for help makes my burden light!

I'll make mistakes my whole life through, but I can grow each time I do!

Session 1

Power Up!

Scripture: Proverbs 1:7, 8, 10; 2:6; 4:6, 7; Matthew 7:24-27; 2 Corinthians 5:17
Power Verse: 2 Corinthians 5:17
Power Point:
With Jesus in my heart to lead the way, I can make wise choices everyday!

Know the difference between wise and unwise choices and where to find the power to follow through with difficult choices.
Feel empowered to make and follow through with choices by relying on God's Word and power for guidance.
Identify difficult decision-making situations and ask God for His wisdom and power to help them through one such situation this week.

Get Into the Game

Before kids arrive, arrange the activity centers. If space is limited, try finding another room such as the church kitchen or a hallway to set up the obstacle course. As students enter, let them rotate among the areas until they complete all three.

Activity #1

Let two to four kids work together at a sand box or an area where a sand castle can be built. If you have a Polaroid camera, take a picture of each castle before a new group arrives. Each group of kids will destroy the previous castle and build a new one. Repeat until all have had a chance to build a castle. Then let the first group go to the box and level the last one.

Activity #2

Arrange an obstacle course by placing several large objects such as tables, chairs, large cardboard boxes, and anything else you can find in such a way that kids have to climb over, crawl under, or pass through objects to get from point A to B. As kids arrive to this center, place them in pairs. One person in each pair is blindfolded and the partner leads him through the course by talking to or physically leading him. When complete, the partners switch roles.

Activity #3

Place pages from a book of mazes (you can find these in the puzzle section of your local bookstore) on a table along with an egg timer. Have kids choose a maze and try to solve it within an allotted time. Display these puzzles around the room.

Materials
sand box, or other area where a sand castle can be built, Polaroid camera (optional), book of mazes, egg timer, large objects to form an obstacle course (tables, chairs, cardboard boxes)

Step 1

Introduce the unit by saying, "Today we are starting a new unit about making choices. You probably don't think about it, but you make choices all the time! Our lives are full of decision-making situations. For instance, let's make a list of how many choices you made already this morning." Guide students to think of as many as possible *(whether or not to get up, brush your teeth, what to eat for breakfast, what to wear, what to do first during the opening activity)*.

"When the choices we make each day are small, we don't think much about them. But each one is important. For instance, how would your morning have been different if you had refused to get up? Or you had not eaten breakfast? Or you had not brushed your teeth? Even though you probably didn't think much about the choices you made this morning, each one determined how well, or poorly, your morning went for you.

"But our choices in life are not always that small or simple. Many are hard to make, and we may wish we didn't have to make them. Some of our choices feel confusing, and we may have trouble deciding what to do! During those times, we can feel as if we're going through an obstacle course blindfolded!" Ask kids to tell how they felt when they tried to make their way through the course blindfolded.

"Sometimes we make a wrong choice, and it gets us into trouble. When working the mazes, if you made one wrong choice, you got stuck. It probably took you a long time to find your way out after making that wrong choice. That's why choices are so important. Every time we make a choice, we either help ourselves or hurt ourselves. During this unit we will talk about how to make more choices that help us. We'll call those wise choices. We'll also discuss choices that hurt us. We'll call those unwise choices. Let's start by seeing what God's Word says about making choices."

Divide kids into three groups and give each group one of the following assignments. They should be prepared to repeat these during Step 2.

1. Proverbs 1:7, 8, 10; 2:6; 4:6, 7. These verses teach the importance of seeking wisdom and knowledge in leading a successful life. This group will prepare a poster depicting how these verses relate to making wise choices in life situations. This can be one picture the group works on together. Or create a collage by letting each student take a verse and draw a picture depicting that verse. Guide kids to think about the meaning of the verse when they make their pictures. For instance, they might draw a child stealing with a circle and line through

Materials
large sheet of paper or poster board, Bibles, markers, paper

it (∅ - no stealing), or a child praying for God's wisdom to know what to do.

2. Matthew 7:24-27—Parable of the Wise and Foolish Builders. Kids will prepare this as a drama to present to the rest of the class. The easiest method is for one or two students to read the passage while the others pantomime the action. Let them creatively find ways to depict the action and to involve everyone.

3. 2 Corinthians 5:17—Power Verse. This group will prepare to teach this verse to the rest of the class by writing it on individual sheets of paper, placing one or two words on each sheet. When it is time to teach the verse, they will distribute the sheets to classmates and arrange the classmates in order in the front of the room. They will lead the class in reading the verse together. Then they will ask two kids to hide their sheets of paper and lead the class in reading it again, filling in the missing words. They will continue until the class can say the verse with no words displayed at all.

Step 2

Ask five volunteers to read the script from page 21. Then lead the kids in a discussion with the following questions.

1. Did Roger make a wise choice? Why or why not?

2. What are some of the possible outcomes of his decision to join the other boys? *(He may get into trouble; he will gain acceptance by the big three.)*

3. In the long run, do you think Roger will be happy with his choice? *(Going against our conscience never makes us happy. Ultimately, Roger made an unwise choice that can only lead to more unwise choices.)*

4. What could Roger have chosen to do differently? *(Walk away.)* Would that have been easier or harder than what he chose? *(It's always harder to stand alone.)*

"As you can see, making wise choices is not easy. Sometimes it takes real strength and power to choose what is right! For Roger, it would have taken more power to say no to the gang than to go with them. We have to learn how to know the right thing to do and where to get the power we need to do it! Let's see what we discovered from our Bible activities that can help us with that."

Invite Groups 1 and 2 to make their presentations at this time. Using these presentations as a guide, compare the difference between wise and unwise choices. Make an overhead transparency from page 22, then ask kids to help you think of statements and examples for each column. The chart on the next page illustrates possible responses.

Materials
photocopies of page 21, photocopy of page 22 made into an overhead transparency, overhead projector, markers

Unwise Choices . . .	Wise Choices . . .
• hurt others (fighting, put downs, name calling, lying, stealing, etc.) • hurt myself (drugs, acting in ways so no one wants to be my friend, disobeying parents, etc.) • destroy property (vandalism, smashing things when angry, breaking someone else's things to get even, etc.) • get me into trouble • disobey God's Word	• help me get along with others • help me stand up for what is right • never violate the teachings of God's Word (This is the main point of Jesus' parable about the wise and foolish builders.) • help others who need help

Reread Matthew 7:24, then say, "The most important rule to remember when deciding what to do is to follow the teaching of God's Word. But there's more to making wise choices than knowing what to do. We must also have the power to do it. Deep down inside, all of us want to be powerful people. Almost everyone loves to watch stories of super heroes on TV or in the movies. We like to imagine that we could do all those powerful actions. But we can't because all those super heroes have something no one else has—a source of power. For instance, where does Superman get his power? Or the Power Rangers?" (Mention other current "power heroes" your kids watch.) "All of those power sources are fantasy, but we like to watch them so we can pretend to be powerful, too! In reality, however, we don't have to pretend to have a power source. God's power is available to help us make wise choices. How do we get God's power in our lives?" *(Inviting Jesus to be our Lord and Savior.)* Invite Group 3 to teach the Power Verse to the kids.

Summarize by saying, "When we invite Jesus to come into our lives, all of God's wisdom and power becomes available to us any time we need it! It's the only true source of power. So no matter how difficult our choices may be, we have a power source to make wise choices!"

Step 3

In each session of this unit, Step 3 will help the kids practice making wise choices. Using the scenario about Roger, let the kids suggest some alternative choices such as the following:

1. Walk away and not say anything to anyone.
2. Walk away and tell a teacher what will happen.
3. Talk to his parents later about the incident.
4. Follow his friend and talk to him about reconsidering his actions.

5. Walk away and talk to his friend later about the wrong choice he made.

Take It to the Next Level

Distribute photocopies of page 23 and give kids a few minutes to fill them out. Invite kids to share which choices they consider the hardest to handle and to explain any difficult decision they are facing. Let this lead you into a prayer time by praying with the kids for God's power to handle their difficult choices. Start a prayer journal for this unit by recording a prayer request for each student in the class (a choice they face, a decision to ask Jesus into their lives, or anything else they suggest) into a notebook. Use this prayer journal to pray for the kids during the week, as well as to lead your prayer times in class each week.

Conclude your session by directing kids' attention to the "Power to Choose" poster (see Unit Introduction for details about making this poster). Explain that you will add Power Points to it each week. These verses and bits of wisdom will help them remember how to take charge of their lives by making wise choices every day. Attach the hockey player (photocopy of page 14) with today's Power Point just in front of the goal on the left.

Materials
photocopies of page 23, pens or pencils, small notebook to track kids' prayer requests, "Power to Choose" poster displayed in a prominent location, photocopies of page 14

Roger's Choice

Characters
Roger, his best friend Jacob, three boys *(the Big Three)*

Props Needed
A can of spray paint *(any aerosol can will do)*

Scene
Roger and his best friend are walking down the school hall.

Roger: Mr. Collins gave me a *D* on my essay! I can't believe it! I worked really hard on it and even had my mom check it!

Jacob: Aw, never mind. Everybody knows Mr. Collins gives the lowest grades in school. I wish he would retire or something.

(The Big Three come up behind Roger and Jacob and surprise them. One of them is carrying a can of spray paint.)

Boy #1: Hey guys, want to help us? We're going to spray paint Mr. Collins' car! *(shows can of paint; all three laugh and huddle together)*

Jacob: *(to Roger)* Hey, it's The Big Three! We've been trying to hang out with these guys for a long time. This is the first time they've ever asked us to do anything with them!

Roger: *(hesitant)* Yeah, but spray paint a teacher's car? That doesn't feel right to me.

Boy #2: Hey! You coming or what?

Jacob: Yea, cool! *(to Roger)* C'mon, Roger, you can get back at Mr. Collins for giving you a *D* on your essay!

Roger: I… I don't know…

Boy #3: Look, we're going, OK? You can come or not! *(All three walk out.)*

Jacob: Roger! This is our big chance! You can blow it if you want, but I'm going!

Roger: But it's wrong!

Jacob: It's not wrong. Mr. Collins is the meanest teacher in school and you know it! You do what you want, but I'm going! *(Runs out)*

Roger: *(Paces back and forth for a second, trying to decide what to do. Then he runs after the boys.)* Guys, wait up! I'm coming with you!

Unwise Choices...	Wise Choices...

Choices, Choices everywhere!

1. Read the following situations. Fill in the blank lines with other situations you and your friends face.
2. Place an X in front of five or more that you feel would be the most difficult or scary for you to handle.
3. Place an O in front of the ones you currently face.
4. Be honest! You won't have to show your list to anyone.

_____ Pressure from friends to do something you feel is wrong.

_____ Handling a younger brother or sister who irritates you.

_____ Handling an older brother or sister who picks on you.

_____ Getting picked on or teased at school.

_____ What to say or do when your divorced parent says something negative about the other parent *(happens a lot when parents are divorced)*.

_____ Cheating on a test—especially when you had a really good reason why you couldn't study.

_____ Getting into fights.

_____ Pressure to join a neighborhood gang.

_____ Having to get along with a step parent you don't like.

_____ Having to get along with a step brother or sister you don't like.

_____ Lying to cover up when you do something wrong.

_____ _____

_____ _____

_____ _____

Think of the **most difficult decision** you have to make now or sometime soon. Write about it in the space below:

_____

_____

_____

Remember that God will give you the wisdom and power to make a wise choice when you ask Him to help!

Session 2
Balancing Act

Scripture: Matthew 14:22-32; Galatians 5:22, 23; James 1:5
Power Verse: James 1:5
Power Point:
When my head and my heart agree, I've found the choice that's best for me!

Know five steps that can help students balance feelings and thoughts when faced with decisions.
Trust their feelings to guide them (when they take time to think about those feelings).
Practice using the five steps by applying them to a specific decision-making situation.

Get Into the Game
Activity #1
Open today's session with a number of simple activities that require balance. Have several activities going at one time so kids can try one and then go to another. Use the following suggestions, or choose some of your own.

1. Balance Beam. If possible, have a low balance beam available. Ask kids to do simple things such as walk across, walk across with arms at their sides, or walk across backwards.

2. Relay. Challenge kids to cross the room by hopping on one foot. This should be fairly easy for most kids. Then challenge them to do it again, this time holding the other foot with their hand. Have them try this in several positions (for example, hold their foot behind them with their right hand, then their left hand, then hold their foot in front of them with the right and then left hand). Each position will change their center of gravity and force them to adjust their balance.

3. Book balance. Have kids take turns walking across the room with a book balanced on their heads. Those who can do that easily can be challenged by doing it again with two books.

4. Stacking Blocks. Have a set of blocks or other items available for stacking. Challenge kids to see how many items they can stack without falling. Caution them to balance their items carefully to get a really high stack.

Materials
a balance beam, medium-sized books, blocks and other items for stacking

Activity #2
Bring a pitcher of Kool-Aid soft drink mix to class using only one fourth the amount of sugar needed. Bring the rest of the sugar to add later. When kids have completed the balancing activities, invite them to have a cool drink. Distribute cups of

Materials
a pitcher of Kool-Aid soft drink mix made with one fourth of the needed sugar, (bring the rest of the sugar to add later)

the drink mix and wait for kids' responses. Taste some yourself and say, "Oh, I must not have gotten the proper balance of water and sugar. It tastes awful!" Add more sugar and let kids have their drink.

Step 1

Begin by briefly reviewing last week's session. Use the transparency you created to review the difference between wise and unwise choices. Then say, "Today we'll talk more specifically about *how* to make wise choices, and we'll see that it's not always as easy as it sounds! Just like all the balancing activities we did earlier, they looked simple, but were not as easy to do as they looked! It takes practice to become skilled at doing balancing activities well. And what was wrong with the drink I brought?" *(The recipe was out of balance; it needed more sugar.)*

"Making wise choices is like our opening activities. First, we have to learn what 'ingredients' go into making a wise choice, and then we have to learn to balance those ingredients. Here's the secret: to make wise choices, keep a proper balance between *thinking* about your choices and listening to your *feelings*.

"That sounds simple, doesn't it? But just like our balance activities, it is not nearly as simple as it sounds. Let's learn more about that, starting with what the Bible tells us about balancing thinking and feeling."

Divide kids into two groups and give each group one of the Bible Search Assignments photocopied from page 30 (cut this sheet apart so each group reads only their own assignment.) Give them time to complete their task, preparing to share their work during Step 2. If your class is large, divide it into three groups and have the third group prepare today's power verse, James 1:5, to teach to the class, just as Group 3 did last week. Check on each group's work, guiding them to the following conclusions:

1. Matthew 14:22-32. Help kids see that by choosing too quickly, Peter wasn't prepared to follow through with the consequences of his choice. When he finally started to think, he became frightened and almost drowned!

2. Galatians 5:22, 23. Help the kids see that the character qualities God gives help us maintain a balance between thinking (self-control, patience, faithfulness, goodness) and feeling (love, joy, peace, gentleness) when making choices. For example, if we have the quality of love, we will not feel good about choices that are unloving. If we have the character quality of patience, we will take time to think before acting. When

Materials
transparency made during last week's session, overhead projector, photocopy of page 30 cut apart, poster board or flip chart paper, markers, Bibles

making a poster, kids can divide it in half, listing qualities that help us think on one side and qualities that help us feel on the other.

Step 2

Begin by reading the following scenario.

Darlene walked into her room and saw the broken figurine immediately. It was an extra special figurine from her Precious Moments collection. It was the one Daddy had given her on her last birthday, right before he moved out of the house. She stormed towards the kitchen where her six-year-old sister was eating a snack. "How dare you come into my room and touch my collection!" she screamed. "I warned you never to come into my room again!" Just then, Darlene noticed her sister's favorite doll laying on the table. Quickly, she picked it up, ripped the head off and threw it down. "There," she said, "now maybe you'll stay out of my room!"

Ask, "Did Darlene make a wise choice?" *(No, using hurtful or destructive actions is never wise.)* "Darlene had a right to feel angry about the broken figurine. But she acted on her feelings only; she did not take the time to think about what had happened. What might have happened differently if she had stopped to think?" *(She might have asked what happened and discovered her sister was not the one who broke the figurine; she could have asked her mom to help with the problem of her sister entering her room; she could have found a safe, non-destructive way to express her anger before talking to her sister.)* "Making a choice based only on feelings led Darlene to make an unwise choice. But making a choice without listening to our feelings at all can also get us into trouble." (Review last week's story of Roger, who chose to go with The Big Three to spray paint a teacher's car.) "What were Roger's feelings telling him about the choice he was making?" *(That spray painting a teacher's car was wrong.)* "But Roger disregarded his feelings and ended up making an unwise choice.

"We can learn more about balancing thinking and feeling from the Bible. Let's find out what we learned in our Bible search activities." Invite kids in Group 1 to make their presentation at this time. Then say, "Even Bible people had trouble balancing thinking and feeling to make wise choices. Since God knows how hard that would be for us, He offers us help." Invite kids in Group 2 to make their presentation, guiding kids to see that we can ask God to give us the fruit of the Spirit in our lives, which will help us balance our thinking and feeling.

Display a well-balanced mobile and demonstrate how it works by pulling on it and watching it regain its balance. Say, "Have you ever thought about how a mobile works? What

Materials
well balanced mobile, a small bag containing marbles or beans

must happen for it to move smoothly, as this one does?" *(All the pieces have to be in the right position so their weight balances each other.)* "A mobile is all about keeping the proper balance. Look what happens if I add some extra weight to one piece." (Attach a small bag of marbles or beans to one piece.) "It doesn't work anymore because one piece is now out of balance. Likewise, if we choose without thinking, or ignore our feelings altogether, we will probably make an unwise choice."

Step 3

Use a flip chart to present this information. Say, "You can balance thinking and feeling by remembering five words when making choices." Write the following words in big letters on the flip chart or poster board, giving the following information about each one.

1. Stop. Don't choose too quickly, especially if you're angry. You don't want to make a choice based on how you feel at the moment.

2. Think. Consider all your choices in this situation. Look for as many as possible; there are always more than you think at first! Consider what the Bible says in every situation.

3. Listen. Pay attention to what your feelings tell you, especially if they say the choice you are about to make is wrong. Feeling uncomfortable about your choice is a warning signal you need to heed.

4. Ask. Seek help if you need it. Sometimes making a wise choice isn't easy. Asking for help is always a wise choice! You can ask parents, other adults, and God to help you find the right choice.

5. Do. Choose the option you believe is right—and do it! Don't forget to ask for help to carry it out, if you need it.

Lead the class in saying these words aloud several times. Ask them to say them louder and stronger. Then take the poster away and have them say them again.

Practice using the steps with the scenario about Darlene. Then guide the students to talk through each of the steps they just learned.

1. Stop—Review the facts of the scenario.

2. Think—List all of the options available to the character and what the Bible says can guide her choice.

3. Listen—What could their feelings tell them about their possible choices? Did the character disregard any uncomfortable feelings?

4. Ask—Did the character need help? Who could have helped? How could God have helped?

5. Do—Agree as a group on a wiser choice the character

Materials
flip chart or poster board, markers, photocopy of page 31 cut apart, poster of James 1:5

could have made. Then choose volunteers to act out the scene, depicting this wise choice.

Divide the kids into two groups (boys and girls would work well) and give each group a role play scenario from page 31. Give the groups time to prepare their role plays, and then ask them to present their skits to the rest of the class. Use the following information to guide students' work.

Group 1. Jeremy chose an action based only on his feelings. Possible alternatives: talk to his Dad on the phone and tell him how he feels; not talk to his dad right now but tell his mom how he feels; ride his bike in a safe area; write a letter to his dad, telling him how he feels.

Group 2. Lucy chose to disregard her feelings when making her choice. Possible alternatives: ask Betsy if she told (maybe the boys saw her paper and Betsy didn't tell); tell Betsy how hurt and angry she felt; do nothing for a while, until she calms down, then decide what to do.

Have kids say the five steps aloud several times again. Display a poster with today's Power Verse, James 1:5, written out. (If you assigned a group of students to teach the verse, invite them to do so). Say, "Here is an important verse to learn and remember. This verse is a direct promise from God to you. It is part of your power source. Asking God to give you wisdom to make wise choices is a great source of power in your life!"

Take It to the Next Level

Using poster board and marker, create two signs, one that says "Feel too much" and the other "Think too much." Tape them to walls on opposite sides of the room. Say, "When you're making a choice, balancing thinking and feeling is not easy. Everyone, including adults, struggles with it. Think for a moment about the choices you make, especially the ones that get you into trouble. Would you say you tend to act without thinking (feel too much) or disregard your feelings and choose actions you know are wrong (think too much)?"

Encourage kids to think about this carefully, honestly evaluate their decision-making style, and then move to the area near the sign that describes their style. You can set the tone for this self-evaluation by telling them your answer to this question and then positioning yourself under the sign that describes you.

Ask kids to remain in these areas as you conduct your prayer time. Use your prayer notebook to review requests from last week, and ask kids to share new ones. As you pray for the class today, stand with the group under the "Feel too much" sign and pray that God will give them His power to think before making choices this week. Then move to the other side and

Materials
two pieces of poster board, markers, prayer notebook, "Power to Choose" poster, photocopies of page 14

ask God to give this group the power to acknowledge, and act on, their feelings, especially if that means standing alone. Finish your prayer time by praying that all the kids would draw on God's wisdom as they make their difficult choices this week.

Conclude the session by directing kids' attention to the "Power to Choose" poster (see Unit Introduction for details about making the power poster). Review last week's Power Points. Attach the hockey player slightly to the left of the center circle with today's power points written on him.

Group 1

1. Read Matthew 14:22-32.

2. Answer these questions:

When Peter made his choice, did he:

    A. Think too much?

    B. Feel too much?

    C. Have a good balance between thinking and feeling?

What was the result of Peter's choice?

3. Prepare a simple skit to present this story to the rest of the class.

Bible Search Assignments

Group 2

1. Read Galatians 5:22, 23.

2. Answer this question:

How many of the character qualities listed in these verses help us think before we make choices? List them here: _____

_____

How many of the character qualities listed in these verses help us use our feelings to make wise choices? List them here: _____

_____

3. Make a poster showing how the character qualities God gives us helps us balance thinking and feeling.

Group 1

Jeremy is sitting on the front step of his house waiting for his dad to pick him up. Jeremy hasn't seen his dad for a month, and his dad promised to take Jeremy camping this weekend to make up for it. His camping gear is all ready, but his dad is two hours late. Then his mom comes out to the porch.

"I'm sorry, Jeremy," she says. "Your dad isn't coming tonight. He's on the phone now and wants to talk to you."

Jeremy feels disappointed, hurt, and angry. "Well I don't want to talk to him!" he screams at his mom. Then he runs off the porch, gets on his bike, and rides away as fast as he can. Without thinking, he rides into the street—just as a car is coming. The driver slams on the brakes and honks the horn. Startled, Jeremy swerves out of the car's path—just in time.

1. Did Jeremy choose by thinking too much or feeling too much?

2. Using the five steps, find at least one better choice Jeremy could have made.

3. Prepare a short skit showing Jeremy acting on this wise choice.

Role Play Scenarios

Group 2

Lucy was horrified that she got an *F* on her math test. She hadn't had time to study because her parents had gone out the night before the test, leaving her to watch her younger sister. By the time her parents had come home, she had been too tired to study. Lucy was embarrassed that math was so hard for her since it didn't seem to be difficult for anyone else. She hid her paper and didn't tell anyone about her grade—except for Betsy, her best friend. But this morning when she got to school some of the boys laughed at her. "Hey Lucy! You dumb or something? That math test was so easy even a first grader could have passed it! Ha ha!"

Lucy felt humiliated and angry. *How could Betsy do such a thing to me!* she thought to herself. *I'll show her! I'm going to tell James Malone that she's in love with him! She'll just die! That will fix her!* For a moment, however, Lucy thought, *that's a mean thing to do, and I shouldn't do it.* But when she saw Betsy coming toward her, she turned and yelled, "Hey James! I have something to tell you!"

1. Did Lucy choose by thinking too much or feeling too much?

2. Using the five steps, find at least one better choice Lucy could have made.

3. Prepare a short skit showing Lucy making this wise choice.

Session 3
Take Charge!

Scripture: Luke 8:42-48
Power Verse: Romans 8:37
Power Point:
When the choice I've made feels hard—
　but it's right,
asking for help makes my burden light!

Know how taking risks and asking for help empowers students to follow through with wise choices that feel difficult or scary.
Feel motivated to take risks and ask for help when acting on choices they know are right.
Make a plan to follow through on at least one difficult choice.

Get Into the Game

Begin today with an indoor version of the game, Steal the Bacon. Divide your class into two teams, and have each team stand on opposite sides of a round table. Place a piece of masking tape across the middle of the table to designate sides. Have teams number off from one up. If the teams are uneven, give two numbers to one person on the larger side. Place an object kids can grab easily in the middle of the table. To play, have everyone take two steps back from the table. Then call out a number. The person on each team with that number approaches the table and tries to grab the object without being tagged by the other person. The two kids whose number was called may approach the table and circle it, but they may not actually touch the table at any time; they must use balance to reach and grab the object. When the object is successfully taken from the table, a point is awarded to that team. If the one taking the object is tagged, no point is awarded. If a stalemate seems to be in progress, you can call a second number to approach the table and assist.

　If a round table is not available, kids can stand in a circle with the object placed in the middle. Proceed in the same way, but be aware that playing the game in a small space without the boundary of the table can result in kids getting too rough. Another option is to play the actual version of the game outside in a large area with the two teams lined up facing each other about twenty-five feet apart and a larger, heavier object for the kids to grab (such as a two liter bottle filled with sand) placed between them.

　After playing for a time, gather kids and say, "We played this game to help us talk about following through with our choices.

Materials

table, masking tape, an object kids can grab easily, such as a cup or beanbag

You probably weren't thinking about choices as you were playing, but you actually made some important ones. What were they?" *(How to approach the object; when the best time would be to try to steal it.)* "In the game, it was one thing to look the situation over and choose a good time to steal the bacon. But then you had to actually do it! What reactions did you have when you got to that point?" *(jumpy, scared to try, excited)* "Did anyone miss an opportunity to steal the bacon because you were afraid of being tagged by the other person who was standing so close to you?" *(Let kids respond.)* "To be successful, you had to take a risk and give it your best shot! Sometimes you made it, and sometimes you didn't, but that's what taking a risk is all about! At times I called a second number. Why did I do that?" *(Because the situation required help.)* "Now let's see how this can help us when we are making choices."

Step 1

Say, "Have you ever made a New Year's Resolution? What are some you've made?" (Let kids respond; include your own examples.) "How many did you keep all year?" *(Share a specific example of one you've made, perhaps repeatedly, and could never follow through on the whole year.)* "What are some common New Year's Resolutions people make?" *(lose weight, exercise more, stop biting their nails, not yell at their kids or siblings)* "The New Year's Resolutions we choose are usually changes we would like to make in our lives but never seem to be able to make. Each year we think, 'Maybe this year I can start fresh, this time I'll stick to it!' But there is a big difference between deciding what to do—making a wise choice—and doing what we decide—following through with the wise choices we've made. In the rest of our class today, we will see that taking risks and getting help are the two keys to following through on the choices we make. But first, let's see what we can learn from an incident that happened in the Bible."

Ask a volunteer to read Luke 8:42-48. Then say, "This is a story about a very sick woman. She had suffered with a blood disease for twelve years, and no one could help her. These verses tell us about a difficult choice she made and how she followed through with it."

Distribute photocopies of the scripts on page 38 and choose the main characters. Have the rest of the class be the crowd. Then have the kids present the script as a play. Run through it once as practice and then talk about the following questions:

1. What choice did the woman make? *(to ask Jesus to heal her)*

2. What barriers did she have to following through with her

Materials
photocopies of page 38, Bibles

choice? *(She was weak, the crowd was big, and in those days, women were kept from approaching men directly in public.)*

3. What risks did she take to follow through with her choice? *(risk of being trampled by the crowd; risk of being punished for touching Jesus)*

4. What was the result of the risks she took? *(She was healed.)*

5. What would have happened if she had not taken the risk to follow through? *(She would have been weak and sickly the rest of her life.)*

Have the class present the play one more time, asking them to portray the feelings that must have been present when this event actually happened. Summarize by saying, "When this woman made a choice and took the risks to follow through, Jesus rewarded her faith and courage. Her story is included in the Bible as an example to us. Now let's discover how we can use faith and courage to follow through with our choices too."

Step 2

Begin by reading the following scenario.

Albert finally got a skateboard for his birthday. Most of the kids in his neighborhood had owned skateboards for years, but his parents hadn't been able to afford one until now. Albert discovered, however, that riding the skateboard was not as easy as it looked. The first few times he fell, the other kids laughed and teased him, and he was embarrassed. But the worst experience was when he tried to follow his buddies as they jumped a curb—he flew off his board and put a gash in his head. That ended his skateboard adventures for the day.

The next morning, his friends came to the house. "Grab your board, Al, and let's go cruising!" they said. But Albert shook his head. "I . . . I don't think so, guys. Not today."

"Why not?" they asked with surprise. "You said you wanted to ride with us more than anything! So what's the problem?"

"I can't today, that's all," Albert lied, "maybe tomorrow." The truth was, he was now scared and didn't want to try riding again. He had decided that riding the skateboard just wasn't worth the effort.

Say, "Albert was having trouble following through with a choice he had made to learn to ride his skateboard. Was that a wise choice?" *(Yes)* "What barriers were keeping him from accomplishing his goal?" *(He was embarrassed; he was afraid of getting hurt again.)* "What new choice did he make as a result of the barriers?" *(riding the skateboard wasn't worth the effort.)* "Was that a wise choice?" *(No. Help kids see that Albert made his choice out of embarrassment and fear, not because*

Materials
photocopy of page 39 made into an overhead transparency, overhead projector, markers, poster of Romans 8:37, words of Romans 8:37 printed out on slips of paper (one word per slip)

he actually couldn't ride the skateboard. He was running away from the problem.) "Like Albert, we get ourselves into situations in which barriers tempt us to not follow through with our choices. Let's think of some examples that kids your age actually face and some reasons why it is hard to follow through."

Use the overhead transparency from page 39 to list kids' responses. Some examples are listed below.

Situations:	Barriers to following through:
• saying no to peers when they ask you to do something wrong • obeying parents when you don't feel like doing what they asked • avoiding fights or name calling when angry • learning something new • getting homework done	• afraid of what others will think of us or of losing friends; feel all alone • don't feel like doing it now • forget to do the right thing when situations arise • what we know we should do seems too hard • it's something we've never done before • don't understand or have enough information about what we're supposed to do

"This is where making wise choices gets difficult. Standing up to peers, or remembering the right thing to do when we feel angry, is not easy for anyone. But remember, we have a power source to help us make, and follow through with, wise choices!"

Display the poster with today's power verse written out and have the kids read it together. Say, "No matter what barriers we face, God promises to help us overcome them." Help the kids memorize this important verse by distributing slips of paper with the words of the verse written out, one word per slip. Give these to the kids in random order. Then have them arrange themselves in the proper order and read the verse together several times.

Step 3

Review the five steps of the decision-making process from last week and have kids say them with you several times: stop, think, listen, ask, do. Distribute slips of paper with the steps printed on them, one step per slip. Be sure every student has a slip. Say, "Let's see if we can help Albert follow through in his situation. Think about the step written on your slip of paper and how Albert can use it to help him now." Give kids a moment to think about their answers. Then ask kids with step

Materials
slips of paper with the words *stop, think, listen, ask* and *do* printed on them, one word per slip

one to respond, then step two, and so on. You may want to write the responses on the board or flip chart. Possible answers:

1. Stop! Albert can determine to face his problem and not just hide from it.

2. Think about his options. Some examples: practicing with the guys, learning how to ride without the other guys around, or asking the guys not to tease him when he falls. Of course, he can also choose to ignore the situation and stay in the house.

3. Listen to his feelings. By listening to his feelings, Albert will realize that he feels fear and embarrassment and that avoiding these feelings will only make him feel worse. What he really desires is to get out there and ride!

4. Ask for help if he needs it. He can start by asking God for courage to do something that feels difficult; he could ask the guys or someone else to teach him the basics; he could ask his parents to get him a helmet and knee pads to protect him.

5. Do it. He can grab the skateboard now and go with the guys, or go later to practice on his own.

Remind kids that whatever Albert decides, it will not be easy to follow through. But if he is willing to take a risk and ask for help if he needs it, he can accomplish his goal of learning to ride his skateboard. Then he can cruise with his friends.

Read the following situation and have the kids think about how they could make a wise choice. Proceed as you did above, only this time have kids exchange slips so they think through how to use a different step of the process.

While you are eating lunch in the school cafeteria on Monday morning, one of your friends asks you what you did over the weekend. Among other things, you mention that you went to Sunday school. Another person at the table hears this and shouts, "You went to Sunday school? Hey everybody! We'd better be good today or this kid will tell God on us! Ha-ha!" Lots of other kids laugh, too.

Here are some possible responses:

1. Stop! Remember not to do anything impulsively. Give yourself time to think before you react.

2. Think about your options. For example, say nothing so the situation won't get worse; say something that will let everyone know that God is important to you; talk to the kid later and tell him you didn't appreciate his comment; start carrying your Bible to school so everyone will know you are a Christian.

3. Listen to your feelings. Your immediate feelings will probably be embarrassment and either fear (to say anything else) or anger (you want to punch him out for making the remark). After thinking about your alternatives, your feelings will tell you if you are making a wise choice or just reacting to one of those feelings. For example, punching the guy out is not a wise choice, nor is ignoring the situation simply because you are embarrassed or afraid. However, ignoring the situation to avoid a fight with a bully may be the wisest choice.

4. Ask for help if you need it. You can start by asking God for wisdom to know what to do and courage to follow through. You could also talk to your parents or Sunday school teacher about the best way to handle situations like this in the future.

Do whatever you feel is the wisest choice.

Take It to the Next Level

Distribute photocopies of page 40 and give kids a few minutes to fill them out. Talk about how they responded to each situation. Which seem hardest for your kids to handle? Keep track of these so you can pray for your students during your prayer time. Then ask for volunteers to talk about the decision-making problem they listed on the bottom of their sheets, the risks they will need to take to follow through, and where they can go for help. Guide them to think of other areas of risk, and sources of help they can add to their sheets.

Use your prayer notebook to conduct your prayer time. Remind kids of God's power to help them follow through on their choices. Have them say Romans 8:37 one more time. Then pray for God to make that power real in the kids' lives this week.

Conclude the session by directing kids' attention to the "Power to Choose" poster (see Unit Introduction for details about making this poster). Review previous Power Points. Attach the hockey player with today's Power Points from page 15 and place him to the right of the center circle.

Materials
photocopies of page 40, prayer notebook, "Power to Choose" poster, photocopy of page 15

A Woman Touches Jesus

Characters: Sara, Ruth, Jesus, Peter, the crowd

Props: Two chairs, headpieces for main characters

Scene 1

(The woman and her friend are seated in the chairs, talking.)

Ruth: *(looks scared)* You can't do this, Sara!

Sara: *(weak)* I have to do this, Ruth. I've tried everything else. Jesus can heal me! He's coming to our town today. I'll never have this chance again!

Ruth: He's just passing through. Besides, you know our laws! Men can't talk to women in public. How will you ask him?

Sara: Other women have found a way to talk to Jesus.

Ruth: But the crowds following Jesus are huge, and His disciples make sure all the women and children stay behind the men. You're so weak you can hardly make it through a day. How will you fight this crowd?

Sara: I may need a friend to help me…

Ruth: Oh no. Not me. *(Gives in)* OK, maybe if we get started now we'll have a chance.

Sara: Thank you, my dear friend. *(They exit, Ruth helping Sara walk.)*

Scene 2

(Sara and Ruth are standing center stage. Everyone else is off stage, with Jesus in the middle.)

Sara: *(Looks toward crowd)* Here they come, Ruth. I see them.

Ruth: But there are so many of them. *(Crowd moves in slowly with Jesus in the center. Crowd members are waving their arms and yelling, "It's Jesus!" "Jesus, please heal me!" "Jesus, free us!" Each crowd member should have a phrase and yell it over and over. As they move to where Sara and Ruth are standing, Ruth is pushed to the back and Sara is knocked down. Ruth is pushed along with the crowd as they move to the side and stop. Everyone crowds around Jesus.)*

Sara: *(on ground)* Oh no, now what will I do? Now I'll never get close enough to Jesus to ask for His help. *(upset)* Dear God, only You can help me. I have to try. *(She crawls toward Jesus, wiggles between the crowd, and touches the shoe or pants hem of Jesus. Instantly, she gains strength, moves away, and stands up.)*

Sara: It worked! Oh, thank you God! I'm strong again! I'm OK!

Jesus: *(above the crowd noises)* Who touched me? *(Crowd gets quiet and people look at each other. They all say, "Not me" and "I didn't do it" several times.)*

Peter: Lord, there is such a big crowd here today. I'm sure lots of people touched you!

Jesus: No, Peter. I felt power go out of me. *(The crowd turns and looks at Sara.)*

Sara: *(terrified, kneels in front of Jesus)* Oh my Lord, forgive me! But I've been sick for so long. I knew only you could help me, but I was afraid to approach you. Then I thought, *Jesus is so powerful. If I can at least get close enough to touch His robe, I could be healed.* And I was. Look at me! *(crowd gasps)* Please, forgive me for my thoughtless act.

Jesus: *(tenderly)* Daughter, your faith has healed you. Go home, in peace!

Sara: Thank you, my Lord! *(She and Ruth hug and everyone exits.)*

Situations:	Barriers to following through:

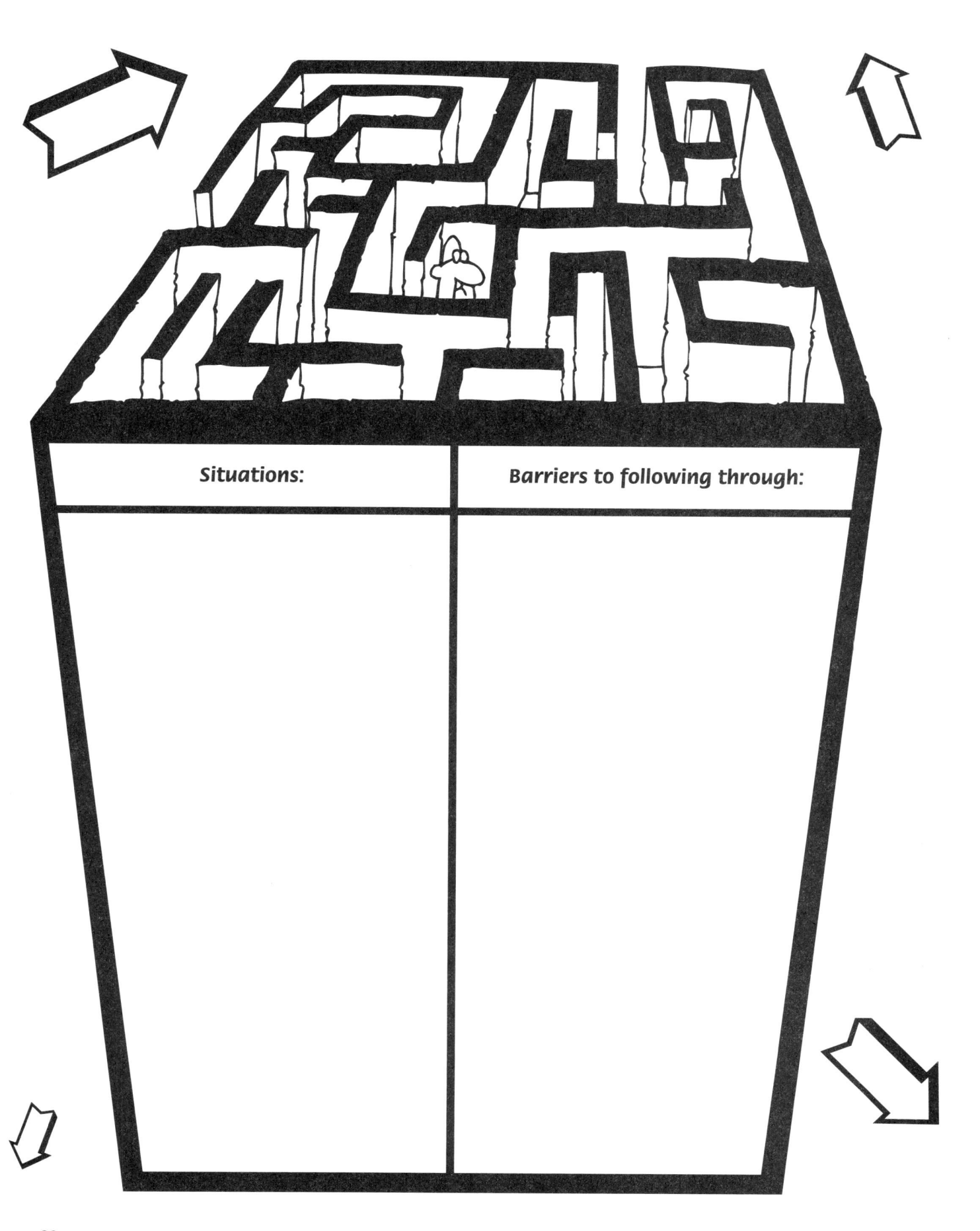

How's My Follow Through?

In the following list, mark the answer that best describes how hard it would be for you to follow through on that choice:

1. You are playing with your friend and your little brother keeps bothering you, wanting to play. Your friend doesn't want him to, but you think it would be OK to let him join the game.
   ____ easy!   ____ hard, but I could do it   ____ I'd need help   ____ I couldn't do it

2. During a math test you see your best friend trying to copy your answers. Since this has happened before, you decide you must talk with her about it after school.
   ____ easy!   ____ hard, but I could do it   ____ I'd need help   ____ I couldn't do it

3. You decide the wisest way to spend your birthday money is on a new computer game.
   ____ easy!   ____ hard, but I could do it   ____ I'd need help   ____ I couldn't do it

4. While visiting your dad for the weekend, he asks you to tell him everything your mom says to you about him. When you say you don't want to talk about your mom, he tells you what he thinks of her and tells you to be sure to tell her what he said. You decide to tell your dad how uncomfortable this makes you feel and ask him to stop doing it.
   ____ easy!   ____ hard, but I could do it   ____ I'd need help   ____ I couldn't do it

5. You decide to buy your sister something special for Christmas even though it would take two week's allowance to get it.
   ____ easy!   ____ hard, but I could do it   ____ I'd need help   ____ I couldn't do it

Following through with our choices is sometimes hard!
Write about one wise choice that's really hard for you to follow through with:
_____
_____

What risks do you have to take to do it?
_____
_____

Who do you know who can help you follow through with it?
_____
_____

Session 4

I Messed Up!

Scripture: Luke 15:11-24; Romans 7:15, 21-25
Power Verse: Romans 8:28
Power Point:
I'll make mistakes my whole life through, but I can grow each time I do!

Know that sometimes everyone makes poor choices and learn how to make wise choices to correct, instead of cover up, mistakes.
Feel forgiveness when they "mess up" and motivation to choose wisely.
Identify past mistakes and choose better ways to handle similar situations in the future.

Get Into the Game:

Have a variety of puzzles and a 100 piece jigsaw puzzle available as kids arrive today. These puzzles should have pieces to manipulate (*not* paper and pencil puzzles) and require the use of trial and error to solve. Encourage everyone to try all the puzzles, including fitting a few pieces into the jigsaw puzzle. Then gather everyone and say, "How many of you were able to solve all, or even one, of the puzzles perfectly the first time you tried? How about the jigsaw puzzle—were you able to place each piece the first time you picked it up? What did it take to solve the puzzles?" *(trial and error, practice)* "How did you feel when you tried to solve a puzzle but made a mistake?" *(Let kids respond.)* "What did you do next?" *(Learned from the mistake and tried something different.)*

"Today we will finish our conversations about making wise choices by talking about what happens when we make a choice and it turns out to be a mistake. We all have times when we make choices that are not very wise because making mistakes is part of being human. We'll learn what to do when we make unwise choices, but first let's see what the Bible teaches us about making mistakes."

Materials
Rubik's Cube puzzles, various puzzles, a jigsaw puzzle with about 100 pieces

Step 1

Divide kids into three groups and give each group one of the following assignments to prepare during Step 2. If your class is small, choose one or two activities for kids to work on during this time.

1. Romans 7:15, 21-25—Paul's struggle with "messing up." This group will prepare a presentation to communicate

Materials
Bibles, large sheet of paper or poster board, markers

41 I Messed Up!

Paul's struggle to the rest of the class. Have kids read the verses and talk about what Paul says in them. Help them see that even Paul, the great Missionary and man of God, struggled with "messing up" from time to time. His words give us encouragement when we make mistakes. Note especially verse 25, in which Paul names his power source for dealing with his struggle—his faith in Christ!

Ideas for presentations: a poster or skit showing scenes of Paul, or kids, making unwise choices and feeling remorse for them; Paul or kids in prayer asking God to help them avoid making unwise choices; kids reading the Bible for guidance. Add titles or captions, such as, "We're human; we make mistakes!" "God gives us power to stop making bad choices." Older kids may enjoy creating a rap depicting the struggle Paul identifies between knowing the right thing to do but feeling pulled to do the wrong thing.

2. Luke 15:11-24—Parable of Prodigal Son. Kids will prepare a drama depicting this story. The easiest way is for one or two students to read the passage while the others pantomime the action. Let them creatively find ways to depict the action and involve everyone. Emphasize the point at which the son realizes he has "messed up" and makes a new, wiser choice.

3. Romans 8:28—Power Verse. Prepare to teach the verse to the rest of the class by writing it on individual sheets of paper, placing one or two words on each sheet. When it is time to teach the verse, students will distribute the sheets to classmates. The classmates will stand in order in the front of the room and lead the class in reading the verse together. Then the student leaders will ask two kids to hide their sheets of paper and lead the class in reading the verse again, filling in the missing words. Continue until the class can say the verse with no words displayed.

Step 2

Begin by reading the following scenario:

Carrie was sitting on her bed holding her stomach. All week she had looked forward to going to the mall with her new friends, Mary Sue and Jackie. But today didn't turn out as she had envisioned! If only we hadn't gone into J.C. Penney's, *she thought.* We never would have seen those dumb sweaters! *They had each found a sweater that they liked, but didn't have enough money left to buy them. As they started to leave, Mary Sue had quietly said, "Look, those sweaters will fit easily into our bags! Let's go take one. They'll never miss three little tops!"*

Carrie had struggled with this, but didn't know how to say no. Besides, she had also found it exciting to sneak back, find a moment when no one was looking and slip the top into her bag. The girls decided to split up and each walk quickly out of the store alone. But when Carrie got to the store entrance, she saw a house detective grab Jackie by the arm and take her away. She hid for a moment, and then snuck out the door and hurried home. She never did see Mary Sue again.

At dinner that night, Carrie felt so awful she couldn't eat. When Mom asked why she wasn't eating, she lied, "I guess we ate too much at the mall today." She then went straight to her room, but had no idea what to do! When the doorbell rang, her heart stopped. She heard Jackie's mother at the door. Her mom called, "Carrie! Come down here, please!" On the way down the stairs, Carrie decided she would simply say, I don't know anything about stealing tops. We all separated for a while (which was true) and when I went to find the others, they were gone. So I came home alone. Mom will believe that, *she thought,* she has to!

Say, "Carrie made a choice in the department store. Was it a wise one?" *(No; stealing is never a wise choice)* "How did she feel about her choice?" *(Sick to her stomach; anxious; scared of being caught)* "Do you think she sees her choice as a mistake?" *(Probably)* "What choice did she make next?" *(lie to cover it up)* "Is that a wise choice?" *(No; lying only makes matters worse.)*

"Let's see what we can learn from Carrie's experience. First, she definitely made an unwise choice—she 'messed up.' We can all relate to that because everyone makes mistakes from time to time. In fact, one of the most encouraging parts of the Bible is that we can learn about many great people who loved God very much and still messed up."

Invite Group 1 to make its presentation at this time. When finished, summarize the passage of Scripture, being sure kids understand the universality of the struggle Paul describes and the power Jesus gives to handle that struggle. Remind kids that our goal is always to make more wise choices and fewer unwise choices, but we will always make mistakes!

Say, "The second thing we can learn from Carrie is the importance of what we do after we make a mistake! Carrie made another unwise choice to try to cover up the first one. What was it?" *(lying)* "What are some other unwise choices we can make to try to cover up our mistakes?" *(hide in our rooms or run away; blame someone else; get into a fight.)* "When we make a mistake, we can either choose to make another unwise choice to cover up the first one, or we can learn from our mistakes and make wiser choices to handle them. Jesus told a story about a boy who did that!" Invite Group 2 to present its skit of the Parable of the Lost Son. When

I Messed Up!

they finish, emphasize the point at which the son faces his mistake and makes a wise choice to deal with it. Ask, "What other choices could he have made that would have made his situation worse?" *(He could have stayed in the pig sty and felt sorry for himself; became a street beggar; started stealing food and money.)*

"In this story the son looked at his mistake honestly and made a wise choice to deal with it. Remember when we talked about taking risks to follow through with the choices we make? What risk did the son take?" *(that his father would not welcome him home and would send him away; that he would be only a servant all his life)* "But what happened when the boy faced his mistake and took a risk to follow through on it?" *(His father welcomed him home and forgave him.)*

"Making mistakes will happen to all of us. Sometimes our mistakes may seem as if they could never be made right, and we may think that we can only try to cover them up. That's when we need to remember our power source!"

Invite Group 3 to teach today's Power Verse to the rest of the class. Summarize it by saying, "Today's Power Verse tells us that God can take any situation, no matter how badly we may think we've messed up, and turn it around for good. The secret is in following the teachings of His Word when we choose what to do next after we've made a mistake."

Step 3

Say, "Let's see if we can help Carrie find a better way to handle her mistake." Review the five steps of the decision-making process and write them on a chalkboard or flip chart: stop, think, listen, ask, do. Have kids say them with you several times. Use these steps to evaluate Carrie's choice and decide what to do about it. Have kids think about Carrie sitting on her bed at the start of the story as you discuss the following:

1. Stop! Carrie is already in a quiet place where she can focus on her problem.

2. Think about the choice she made. She can ask herself, "Did I make a wise choice? Did I follow God's Word? Can I feel good about telling my parents about what I did? Would I make the same choice again in a similar experience, or would I make a different choice?"

3. Listen to her feelings. Carrie's feelings of anxiety and discomfort will tell her she did something wrong. She will also realize that she feels afraid about what will happen next and must not let that fear lead her to another unwise choice.

4. Ask for help if she needs it. She can ask God for wisdom to know the right thing to do, and courage to follow through

Materials
chalkboard or flip chart

with it. She could also ask her mom to help her choose what to do next.

5. Do it. She can now determine to make a wise choice to get out of this situation instead of trying to cover it up.

Say, "Let's help Carrie think about a better choice to get out of this situation." Review the five steps again to determine what Carrie could do next. Give particular attention to how the Bible can help her know what to do. Include the following information in your discussion:

1. Stop! Carrie's first impulse will be to cover her mistake so no one will find out about it. She must stop when she catches herself thinking like that and ask herself what the Bible says is right to do in this situation. If she asks this question, she will see that telling a lie to cover her mistake cannot be right. She should give herself time to think about other choices.

2. Think about the options open to her. Examples: go downstairs and tell her mom and Jackie's mom the truth; ask to see her mom alone before facing Jackie's mom. Later, she can choose to take the top back to the store and pay for, or return, it.

3. Listen to her feelings. All of Carrie's choices will be difficult. She can ask herself, "What do I believe God wants me to do, even if it's hard?" When she makes a choice that is in line with the teachings of God's Word, her feelings will tell her she is doing the right thing. Even though she still feels some fear and anxiety, she will know that she is making the wise choice.

4. Ask for help if she needs it. She can ask God for wisdom to know the right thing to do and courage to follow through with it. She can also ask her mom to go with her to the store to return the top.

5. Do it. She can now take the first step by telling her mom the truth.

Take It to the Next Level

Have kids personalize today's session by reading the following situations. Ask them to think honestly about their answers to the following two questions. Encourage them to share their answers with the rest of the class, but let them pass if they don't want to share this personal information.

1. What unwise choice would you be tempted to make to cover this mistake?

2. By following God's teachings, what wise choice would you make instead?

Read the following situations:

1. While you were baby-sitting, you accidentally broke a valuable figurine. You decide to hide the pieces in your

Materials
"Power to Choose" Poster displayed in a prominent location, photocopy of page 15, prayer notebook, photocopies of pages 47 and 48, scissors

backpack and dump them in the garbage on your way to school tomorrow.

2. You are staying overnight with a friend whose parents decide to take you to an R-rated movie you know your parents do not want you to see. You decide to go and hope they don't find out.

3. Your friends start teasing a kid in your class who everyone thinks is weird. You also think the kid is odd, but the teasing is mean, and the kid is deeply hurt by it. However, you go along with the rest of the kids.

4. Think of an unwise choice you have made recently. How did you cover this mistake? What can you do now to handle this mistake and follow God's teachings in this situation?

Summarize your discussion by reminding kids that God can take any mistake we make and give us the wisdom and courage we need to make it right. Then direct students' attention to the "Power to Choose" poster and attach the hockey player with today's Power Points from page 15. Place him next to the right hand goal.

Distribute photocopies of pages 47 and 48. Be sure to copy the pages onto heavier card stock. Have kids cut the verses and Power Point Cards apart. They can take these home as a reminder of God's power to help them make and follow through with wise choices. End the unit with a prayer time, asking God to guide your students to make wise choices in the situations they face every day.

Power Point Cards

Power Point:

With Jesus in my heart to lead the way, I can make wise choices everyday!

Power Point:

When my head and my heart agree, I've found the choice that's best for me!

Power Point:

When the choice I've made feels hard —but it's right, asking for help makes my burden light!

Power Point:

I'll make mistakes my whole life through, but I can grow each time I do!

©1997 by The Standard Publishing Company. Permission is granted to reproduce this page for ministry purposes only—not for resale.

Power Verse Cards

Power Verse:
"Therefore, if anyone is in Christ, he is a new creation; the old has gone, the new has come!" (2 Corinthians 5:17).

Power Verse:
"If any of you lacks wisdom, he should ask God, who gives generously to all without finding fault, and it will be given to him" (James 1:5).

Power Verse:
"No, in all these things we are more than conquerors through him who loved us" (Romans 8:37).

Power Verse:
"And we know that in all things God works for the good of those who love him, who have been called according to his purpose" (Romans 8:28).

Bridge the Gap

Choosing as a Family

Scripture: James 1:5; Romans 8:37

Know how to work as a family to make wise choices that strengthen the quality of their lives together.
Feel empowered to make wise choices as a family.
Work as a family to make one choice and sign a family contract to carry it out.

Get Into the Game

Activity #1
Have a table with name tags and items to decorate them—such as stickers and rubber stamps—for participants to make their own name tags. Encourage them to decorate their tags with items that have some meaning to them, such as a sticker or stamp of a favorite food or animal.

Activity #2
Families may enjoy doing this session at a time that includes eating a meal together. Have the tables set up and drinks available and let the families bring the food. If families don't know each other very well, you can place conversation starter questions on the tables. Some examples follow:

1. Tell everyone at the table one unique thing about yourself.
2. What is the best thing that happened to you this week?
3. If you could go anywhere in the world, where would you go?

Activity #3
Provide the puzzles you used in **Session 4** and let families work together to try to solve them.

Materials
name tags, stickers, rubber stamps, markers, puzzles used in **Session 4,** arrangements for a family potluck dinner (optional)

Step 1

(NOTE: If you have some students whose parents are not present, help them feel more comfortable by inviting them to explain the poster and teach the verses.) Distribute photocopies of page 53 to parents. Briefly cover the main points. Then invite some students to come forward and tell parents about the "Power to Choose" poster. Lead the group in reading the verses and slogans aloud.

Say, "Today we will discuss how to make wise choices as a family. There is a difference between making an individual choice and working together as a family to make a choice. The more people involved, the more difficult choices become. Yet, making wise choices together is an important part of family living. Let's begin by learning two Scripture verses from this unit that can guide your family to make wise choices."

Invite several students to teach the two verses to the group as they did in **Sessions 1 and 4** of this unit. Summarize, "These verses contain God's promise to give us the two things we need most when making choices: wisdom to know the right thing to do and the power to follow through when the right thing to do is difficult or scary."

Materials
"Power to Choose" poster, slips of paper with the words of James 1:5 and Romans 8:37 printed on them (one or two words per slip), photocopies of page 53

Step 2

Give each family a copy of page 54 and some markers. Place kids without parents into their own group. Say, "Let's begin by making some choices about what we believe to be the best part of our family." As a family, they must agree on the following items to write or draw onto their papers.

1. The thing we most like to do together as a family.
2. The best quality of our family. (*We're fun; we love each other; we have great talks.*)
3. One thing we could all work on to make our family better.
4. One place we would all like to visit.

Visit families as they work, reminding them that they must all agree on their items. When all finish, ask volunteers to share their answers with the rest of the group. Then ask, "How many of you had difficulty making a family choice?" *(Let them respond.)* "Making choices together sounds easy, but it can be hard, even when we're discussing simple things about our family! Solving difficult family problems can be even harder. Let's see how the five steps of making wise choices help."

Materials
photocopies of page 54, colored pencils or markers

Step 3

For this activity, place all participants into groups so that the families are not together. Have them number off, but be sure

Materials
chalkboard or flip chart with the five steps written out

Choosing as a Family

that the parents are equally divided among the groups. Then read the following scenario:

It was report card day at the Smith household. Amy brought her card into the living room. Dad looked at Amy's card—all C's with one D. Mr. Smith knew his daughter could do much better. She had complained all year that she didn't like her new middle school, so he thought she was using this as an excuse not to work. He looked sternly at Amy and said, "This is getting worse instead of better. You're not even trying, Amy."

"Dad, I'm trying really hard! But the work is harder, and the older kids are so mean to the sixth graders that sometimes I don't even want to walk in the halls! I don't know what to do!" Amy hoped Dad would see that she was telling the truth.

"I don't want to hear your excuses!" Dad bellowed. "Go to your room and start your homework. And no TV or going to Marie's house this whole next term!"

Amy was horrified! "Dad, you're not listening to me! I am trying! It's too hard. You can't punish me this way!"

"Yes, I can. Go to your room right now."

Amy stomped to her room and started to cry. She had no idea how to get her Dad to listen to her. When her mom came in a few minutes later Amy said, "Mom, I'm doomed! Dad will never listen to me, and I'll never get better grades in school."

"Maybe we can find a way to solve this problem, Amy." Mom's face was worried but her voice was calm. "Now that he's calmed down, let's go talk to Dad together."

Ask each group to use the five steps to talk about how Amy and her parents can make wise choices and develop a plan to help Amy improve her grades. Instruct the groups to be sure everyone listens to each other's point of view as they talk. Rotate among the groups to help them keep their discussions on track. After ten minutes, focus everyone's attention to the chalkboard or flip chart and ask groups to report on their conversations. Here are some examples of how this family could use the five steps to solve this problem:

1. Stop! As the first principle of making family choices, all members need to listen to each other. Amy's mom had the right idea to get together to talk once feelings had calmed. Dad needs to explore the possibility that Amy's unhappiness at school is a bigger problem than he thought, and Amy needs to realize that getting past this roadblock is vital.

2. Think about their options. The Smiths can start with the question, "How can we solve this problem?" Without criticism, all family members can brainstorm possible solutions. For example, the parents can help Amy with homework to determine where she may need extra help; they can check out what Amy means when she says the big kids pick on the sixth graders; they can find more appropriate ways to help Amy learn study skills than cutting out all TV and seeing her best friend. Amy can tell her parents exactly what bothers her about school; she can suggest ways to focus on her studies that would work for her.

3. Listen to their feelings. To make wise family decisions, all members must learn to listen to each other's feelings. Amy's parents need to listen to Amy's feelings about her difficult transition to middle school, and realize she feels paralyzed by the change. Amy needs to take seriously her parents' concern for her future and their determination that she improve her grades.

4. Ask for help if they need it. The families can begin by asking God for wisdom to know what to do (James 1:5) and power to follow through with it (Romans 8:37). They can also ask for help from school officials, and Amy can ask her parents for help to follow through in learning new study habits.

5. Do it. They can make a specific plan and keep each other accountable to follow it.

Summarize this discussion by stating that making wise choices as a family is hard work, but can improve family relationships and give kids valuable practice in making wise choices in their own lives.

Take It to the Next Level

Ask families to get together again and give each family a photocopy of page 55. Say, "One of the best choices families can make is to play together. Having fun together is the best way to strengthen your family relationships." Instruct them to use the five steps to guide their discussion and arrive at a choice for a family outing. Have all members sign the agreement, and encourage them to actually follow through with it.

End your session with prayer, asking God to give each family wisdom to make good choices and the power to follow through with them.

Materials
photocopies of page 55

Here's What We've Been Learning...

"I had to do it! I didn't have any choice!"

How many times have you heard your kids say those words? How many times have they gotten into trouble because they actually believed those words? As your preteens enter a time in their lives when acceptance by the group is all important, they become especially vulnerable to the belief that they have no choices. Without thinking, they often base their choices on what the group wants to do, rather than on what they believe to be right.

In this unit, our goal was to empower your kids by teaching them a five step process to make decisions following the teachings of God's Word and their own hearts. We also presented the truth that they are not alone when making difficult choices; God promises to give them wisdom to choose wisely and power to follow through with difficult, but right, choices. Finally, we talked about how to evaluate the results of their choices with the goal of accepting and correcting—not covering up—mistakes they made.

Here is a summary of the five steps we taught your kids:

1. Stop. Don't choose too quickly, especially if you're angry. You don't want to make a choice based on how you feel at the moment.

2. Think. Consider all your choices in this situation. Look for as many as possible; there are always more than you first think! Think, too, about what the Bible says that can help you make a wise choice.

3. Listen. Pay attention to what your feelings tell you, especially if they say you are about to make a wrong choice. Feeling uncomfortable about a choice is a warning signal you need to heed.

4. Ask. Seek help, if you need it. Sometimes making a wise choice isn't easy. Asking for help is always smart! You can ask parents, other adults, and God for advice.

5. Do. Choose the option you believe is right—and do it! Don't forget to ask for any help you may need to carry it out.

Scriptural Principles Used in This Session

2 Corinthians 5:17—Having Jesus in our hearts is the starting point of powerful decision making.

James 1:5—God promises to give us wisdom when we are faced with difficult choice making situations.

Romans 8:37—We can conquer any situation when we trust Jesus to help us see it through.

Romans 8:28—God can work all things together for good when we honestly face our mistakes and ask God to help us choose wisely to make it right.

Family Time

The thing we most like to do together as a family:	The best quality of our family:
One thing we could all work on to make our family better:	One place we would all like to visit:

Let's Play!

Brainstorm ideas for a family play time. Be sure everyone contributes ideas. Here are a few examples to get you started:

- *Play games at home with popcorn or other favorite family snacks.*
- *Go to your favorite ice cream shop for a cone or sundae.*
- *Go on a picnic.*
- *Visit an amusement park.*

Write your ideas here: _____
_____
_____

As a family, make a choice and write it here: _____
_____

Plan the details:
    Day: _____
    Time: _____
    Will we invite anyone to play with us? _____
    Other details we need to plan: _____

Make a commitment to do it!
    We, the _____ *(family name)* agree to play together by _____ *(event you planned)* on _____ *(day)*. We promise to carry out our plan and do our best to have a great time together!

        Signed: _____
                _____
                _____
                _____
                _____

Go to Extremes

Choosing to Serve

Scripture: John 15:17; Matthew 25:34-40

Know that serving others is a conscious choice we make in obedience to God's Word.
Feel motivated to plan and participate in a project to serve others.
Carry out a service project.

The heart of this session is to involve your class in the process of choosing a service project to carry out. Before this session, you will need to create a list of projects to suggest to your class. A list of suggestions follows, but feel free to research other possibilities in your church or community. Make your preparations far enough in advance to have representatives from several possible projects give your kids information about projects they could do. Ask representatives to bring pictures (if applicable) of the people they work with and describe to your kids how they could help serve these people. Here are some examples of possible projects:

   1. Aid a local service agency. Food or clothing closets, community centers, and homeless shelters are examples of agencies that may be able to use your class's help. Many of them will have specific projects and will be happy to send a representative to speak to your class.

   2. Project to serve the elderly. Retirement centers can provide you with service projects. Or, your kids may enjoy going to the homes of elderly people in your church to help with chores such as raking leaves or washing windows. Check with your church board or staff for ideas.

   3. Project to serve small children. Check with local day care centers or preschools for suggested projects. You can also check with the person who runs the preschool children's ministry at your church. Your class could raise money to buy toys or other items for nurseries or toddler rooms, or they could serve as assistants during service times.

4. Project around the church. Ask your minister for ideas on how your kids can serve your church. Possibilities include joining a work day, making decorations for a special church emphasis (missions, stewardship, etc.), or raising money to purchase something needed in the building.

Get Into the Game

In advance, prepare a set of cards that will spell out John 15:17, placing only one letter on each card. Pin these to a bulletin board or tape them to the wall in order, with the letters facing the wall. To play, let kids take turns guessing a letter. If the letter is in the verse, reveal the card. Continue letting the kids guess letters until they guess the verse.

Say, "Jesus gave this command before He died on the cross. It is just one verse in the Bible that commands us to love others. Let's look at something else Jesus taught us." Ask one or two volunteers to read Matthew 25:34-40. "These verses tell us something very important about God's heart. They tell us that He cares about the needs of people so much that he considers any service to them as actually caring for Him! Something so simple as giving someone clothes or food or visiting them in the hospital or prison is very important in God's eyes. This is important for us because in our society today, we learn more about taking care of our own needs and getting what we want than about caring for others. God instructs us to make choices about putting others' needs before our own. Choosing to serve others is an important part of being a Christian and loving God. We'll end this unit by making a choice to serve others together."

Materials
3" x 5" cards, Bibles, markers, push pins or tape

Step 1

Say, "There are so many ways we can carry out God's instructions to care for the needs of others. Let's learn about some of them." Invite representatives from local agencies, or ministers or lay leaders from your church to make their presentations to the kids at this time. Keep these presentations short, specific, and include pictures where possible. Add other projects your kids might consider.

Materials
guests to present various project ideas

57   **Choosing to Serve**

Step 2

Distribute photocopies of page 60. Display the diagram and fill it in by asking kids to brainstorm all the ideas they can think of for possible projects. Include all the ones you heard about today, and ask kids to think of others. You may be surprised at how creative they can be! Have them write these on their sheets as you write them on the diagram. When you have written down all the options, ask kids to choose by answering the following questions:

1. Are there any projects we would not be able to complete? *(Too hard; takes too much time or money?)*
2. Are there any you really don't want to do? *(Look for projects the class as a whole does not seem interested in.)*
3. Which two would you most like to do? *(Ask each class member to vote for his two favorites and keep score on your diagram.)*

Now look at the two projects that got the highest votes. Ask the class to vote between those two to determine your final selection.

Materials
photocopies of page 60, chalkboard or flip chart with the diagram from page 60 enlarged, pens or pencils

Step 3

Spend the rest of your class time planning the next steps of your project. Have kids fill in their sheets as you plan as many details as possible. Details to discuss:

1. What advance preparations do we need to complete? *(Make items to give to nursing home residents; raise money; shop and wrap gifts; plan a party for homeless kids; contact elderly for days to rake their leaves. Be sure to send a letter to the parents describing the details of the project, with a permission slip for them to sign and return.)*
2. When can we meet to work on preparations?
3. Who can we ask to help us accomplish this project? *(agency representatives or church leaders; parents to drive; businesses to donate supplies.)*
4. When will we carry out the project?
5. How will we celebrate when it's completed?

When you have done as much planning as you can, close with a time of prayer, asking God to bless your project and work through your kids to meet the needs of others.

Take It to the Next Level

On the day you carry out your project, include a time for debriefing and for celebration after the kids complete their project. Gather everyone together to talk about their experiences,

Materials
refreshments, games

58 **Choosing to Serve**

giving them an opportunity to talk about what they saw, how the people responded to their gifts or presentation, and what they learned about serving others. When they have said as much as they want, end with a prayer for the people they served and ask God to help your kids develop a lifelong habit of serving others.

Conclude with refreshments and play some games together.

Choose to Serve

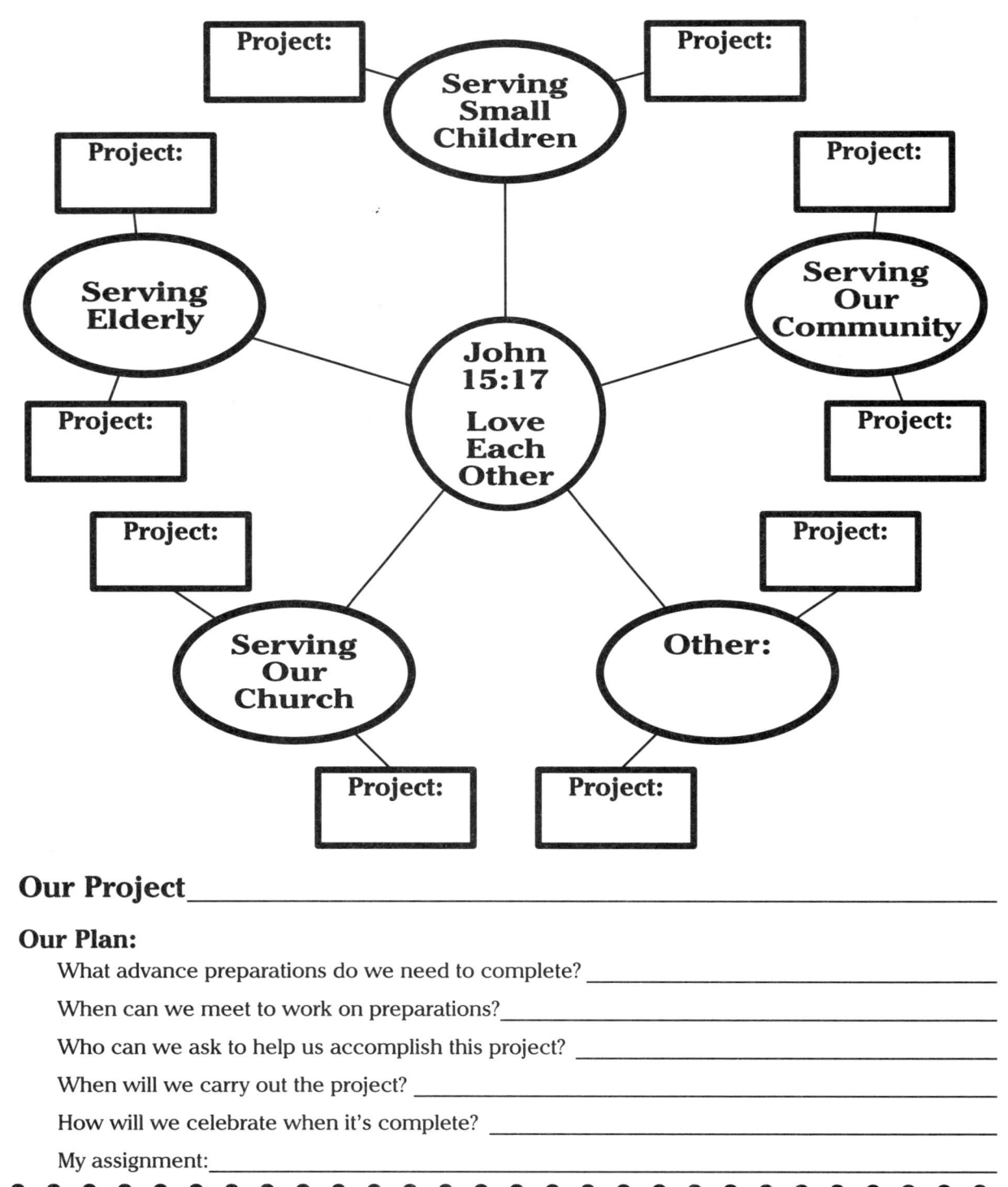

- Project:
- Serving Small Children
- Project:
- Project:
- Serving Elderly
- Project:
- Serving Our Community
- Project:
- John 15:17 Love Each Other
- Project:
- Project:
- Serving Our Church
- Other:
- Project:
- Project:

Our Project _____

Our Plan:
What advance preparations do we need to complete? _____
When can we meet to work on preparations? _____
Who can we ask to help us accomplish this project? _____
When will we carry out the project? _____
How will we celebrate when it's complete? _____
My assignment: _____

Unit 2

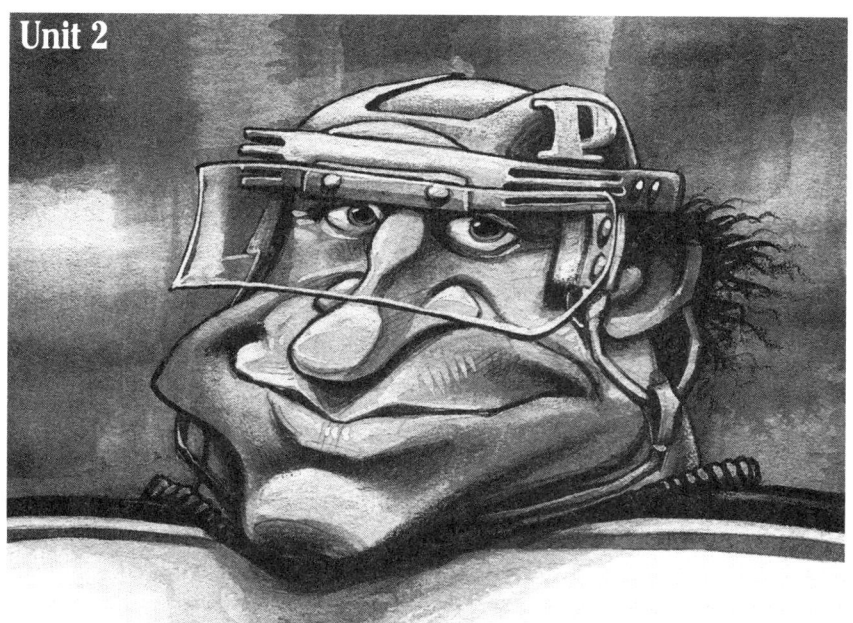

God-Pleasing Power

This unit will encourage preteens to examine the influence their decisions and actions have on others. They will not only explore ways in which godly decisions affect their own relationships with God, but how those same decisions impact their families, their peers, and the worldly society they encounter. The unit will begin with an awareness of how they lead others through their actions and behavior. They will also explore the consequences of positive decisions related to time, money, and speech. The family session will involve an open examination of feelings and priorities that might cause preteens to make poor decisions. Finally, an ongoing "game plan book" will document the results of serving a world that does not expect to be served.

Unit Objectives

Know that they are not too young to have an impact on others.
Feel the positive effects of making wise, personal decisions.
Make a plan for improving one's own example by serving others.

Unit Scripture

The Scripture underlying this unit is found in 1 Timothy 4:12: "Let no one look down on your youthfulness, but rather in

Session 1
Know that God expects all of us to lead others through example.
Feel the impact of effective leading.
Develop a list of ways in which young people can lead through service.

Session 2
Know the difference between wants and needs.
Feel a need for spiritual gifts instead of earthly things.
Commit personal resources to God.

Session 3
Analyze use of personal time.
Examine time from God's perspective.
Commit weekly time for God.

Session 4
Examine the power of words.
Feel the emotional impact of God's Word.
Use words in a positive way.

speech, conduct, love, faith and purity, show yourself an example of those who believe." This verse is used as the focus of **Session 1** and should be used periodically throughout the other sessions as a review and to keep the lessons on focus.

A wise teacher uses as many ways as possible to make the Bible real to students. Here are just a few suggestions:

1. Use the Scripture as memory work and offer a reward to those who can recite it the following week.

2. Write the words from the Scripture on cards, randomly give them to students, and then ask students to arrange themselves in the correct sequence.

3. Use choral or responsive readings.

4. Write the Scripture in modern language, or let the students paraphrase it in words they would use.

5. Add music to the verse or make it into a rap.

6. Play charades and act out each word in the verse.

7. Create a people picture that illustrates the Scripture. This can be done by placing students (with or without) costumes into a still diorama that depicts the verse.

8. Use a "fill in the blanks" work sheet.

9. Have a graffiti wall in which students write the Scripture on poster board and comment about it.

10. Make a Scripture bulletin board that changes each week. The bulletin board can be illustrated by the students themselves.

About the Sessions

Session 1 sets the tone for the unit by asking the question: **Leaders or Followers?** This is particularly meaningful for Christian preteens who struggle to be part of a group that may not always have Christian values and desire to be leaders making a difference for Jesus.

They are introduced to the concepts of leading and following by performing two tasks. They will discover that leading is actually easier than following. They should also realize that following is difficult with an imperfect leader, and that the only true leader is Jesus.

A case study in this session helps the students look for solutions in a difficult situation. It also uses brainstorming to point out that a problem may have more than one answer. The selection of one best solution will help them recognize that all ideas are not equal. By using groups in this activity, the preteen will see that another group may devise another solution to the same situation, and that both might be equally good. Finally, using the story of Timothy as a biblical example they should see that the Bible is a real book with current answers for a complex world.

Session 2 begins by asking each preteen what four items he would save if his home were being threatened by some natural disaster. The students will then divide into groups and locate items from catalogs and magazines that they would label *needs, wants,* or *stuff.* Not everyone will agree on each item, and the teacher must let each group settle its own differences. After telling why he would label a certain item a want, a need, or just stuff, each student will review his own list of items and privately decide what he values most: needs, wants, or stuff.

After focusing on material possessions, the students will be directed to those needs that are spiritual and can only come from God. They will use their Bible skills as they "discover" a list of God's gifts to His people.

Session 3 examines the perspective that, in our society, time is a commodity that is bought, sold, saved, and wasted. It encourages preteens to value their time as a resource and as a gift from God that can be given to others.

In this session, students are placed in "Pair Power" groups to analyze time. "Pair Power" groups may be assigned by the teacher or might be left to the students' choices. Be alert, however, to the preteen who may feel left out. Be sure that he or she is paired with another student as quickly as possible. In fact, you might create a more powerful group called "Triple Power Play."

Again, in both **Sessions 2 and 3,** the student is asked to make personal choices. In **Session 2,** he analyzes his spending habits. In **Session 3,** he looks at his time usage and makes a plan to have more time for God.

Session 4 examines the power of words. Since preteens are surrounded by peers who use bad and unedifying language, this session is particularly meaningful. Students will look at how language is used in both positive and negative ways. Hopefully, they will discover that positive language is much more powerful than negative language. They will also receive an opportunity to write and deliver a dialogue using Scripture as a guide. Finally they will illustrate a word that will become part of their "Godly Vocabulary."

Beginning in **Session 1,** preteens will be asked to become CIA (Christ in Action) Agents, performing secret services each week. They will be given a Secret Service Journal in which to record their actions. The success of this ongoing service project will depend on the teacher. Be as melodramatic as possible when giving the students their secret service assignments. Remember, this is an opportunity for the students to be involved in "make-believe" that will result in a real life adventure.

Many of the problems that preteens have with their parents center around the issues that are part of this series of sessions: leading or following, time, money, and language. The **Bridge** the Gap session will offer parents and preteens an opportunity to examine these points of contention in a loving and accepting environment. First, they will examine the story of Jesus and His parents in Luke 2 by changing roles. Parents will look at the story from the preteen's viewpoint, and the preteen will view it from the parent's perspective. They will then look at each of the issues from both their own viewpoint and from that of the other. By openly sharing ideas, they may find the issues are more related to communication than to poor habits. Finally, each family will make a very specific pledge that will enable the family to be more "of one mind in Jesus Christ."

Secret Service Journal

The Secret Service Journal is a service project designed to be used with four sessions in this unit entitled God-Pleasing Power.

In **Session 1, Leaders or Followers,** the teacher will call each preteen to be a CIA (Christ in Action) Agent. This should be done with as much drama as possible (trench coat, tape recorded message, and lots of secrecy). Students will be asked to keep a "Secret Service Journal" as they accomplish their chosen service. Their mission, should they choose to accept it, will be to secretly do something for someone else each day. They will be asked to record the deed in their journal and then keep a record of what happened as a result of the secret service. They will be encouraged to look for ways to serve that may be out of the ordinary, such as mowing an elderly neighbor's lawn when he is away from home, eating lunch with the classmate who always seems to be alone, writing an appreciation card to a teacher, polishing Dad's shoes after he is asleep.

In **Session 2, Needs, Wants, or Stuff,** time is allowed for sharing the secret service of the past week. At the same time, a second mission is assigned to the CIA agent that should involve a monetary service of some type.

In **Session 3, Time: A Commodity or Resource?**, the CIA agent is asked to render a service that involves the use of time in a special way.

In **Session 4, A Word Is Worth How Much?**, the task involves language as a service. Students are given an opportunity to praise and encourage others.

Sharing among this age group encourages others and also gives them ideas of ways they, too, might serve. However, if the students are uncomfortable with sharing, you may simply want to share your own experiences and ask for ideas of ways others might serve. Try to read the Scripture each week so that it becomes very familiar to the class.

The Power of Prayer

God promises wisdom to those who ask. Prepare for these sessions by spending private prayer time with God, asking Him for the wisdom to make His word meaningful in the lives of the preteens who will be in your class. Pray specifically about each topic as you prepare for that session that you might be a role model for your students. Then pray specifically for each student. Ask God to make each a leader who will be able to use his or her time, resources, and communication skills for Him.

"But if any of you lacks wisdom, let him ask of God, who gives to all men generously and without reproach, and it will be given to him. But let him ask in faith without any doubting, for the one who doubts is like the surf of the sea driven and tossed by the wind" (James 1:5, 6).

Session 1

Leader or Follower?

Scripture: 1 Timothy 4:12

Know that God expects all of us to lead others through example.
Feel the impact of effective leading.
Develop a list of ways in which young people can lead through service.

Get Into the Game

Arrange the chairs into pairs throughout the classroom. Assign students to each set of chairs and explain that they will experiment to determine whether it is easier to follow or lead.

For the first activity, have the students face each other. One student is to pretend he is looking into a mirror. The other student will project a mirror image of the first student. Instruct the student looking into the mirror to pretend to do some of the things people do in front of a mirror (comb hair, brush teeth, put on makeup, shave, make faces). The mirror image is to copy what the person is doing, remembering that a mirror image is actually reversed. After a couple of minutes, have the students switch roles.

During the second activity, the students should sit back to back. One is designated an "artist" and given a sheet of paper and a marker. The second is given a slip of paper with the name of a simple object. This student must instruct the "artist" how to draw that object without revealing what the object is. Some suggestions might include a heart, a house, a triangle, a hamburger, a smiley face, or a book. Again, switch roles so that each student can give and follow instructions.

Discuss whether it was easier to be the leader or the follower. In most cases, the students will agree that it is easier to lead because the leader knows what he will do next. For those who might argue, for example, that following means less responsibility, help them see that unless we attempt to follow God's image and directions, we may find ourselves reflecting the world and drawing a distorted picture.

Materials
chairs, paper, markers, slips of paper with objects to draw

Step 1

Combine students into groups of four. Tell them you are going to read a short story about a young man in a difficult situation. Let each group think of ways to solve this dilemma.

Once a young preacher had served for some time under an older preacher who was known for his ability to lead people to Christ. However, the day came when the young man had to begin his own ministry, and he began working in a situation in which most of the members of his congregation were much older than he was. Even non-Christians in the community were older. Most thought the preacher was too young to lead them. How could he show these people that he had something to offer them?

After reading the case study, give each group these instructions:

First, select a recorder and brainstorm for five minutes (or longer, if time allows) as many ways as the group can think of that will help the young preacher be accepted.

Second, choose the best idea from the brainstorming list.

Third, compose a telegram (letter, notes or e-mail message) to the preacher with the group's advice.

Have each group read the telegram to the entire class. If time allows, you might want to compare similarities and differences in the advice.

Materials
paper, pens or pencils

Step 2

Write the following Scriptures on the chalkboard: 1. Acts 16:1-3; 2. Romans 16:21; 3. 1 Corinthians 4:17; 16:10; Philippians 2:19; 1 Thessalonians 3:2; 4. 1 Timothy 1:3; 5. 1 Timothy 5:1, 2; 1 Timothy 4:12. Prepare index cards with each of the following sentences written on a separate card.

1. Young Timothy becomes Paul's companion and student.
2. Paul calls Timothy a fellow worker.
3. Paul sends Timothy as his messenger to the churches.
4. Timothy goes to Ephesus to minister to the church.
5. Timothy is instructed on how to treat people of all ages.
6. Paul tells Timothy what he should do.

Tell the students that the case study they heard was based on a true story about a young man named Timothy. They will learn more about this young servant.

Distribute Bibles and ask volunteers to find the Scriptures listed on the chalkboard. Then distribute the sentence cards to six students. As the student reads the first sentence ask, "Which one of you has the Scripture that supports that fact?" Continue until all Scriptures and sentences are matched.

Materials
Bibles, index cards, chalk and chalkboard

Reread 1 Timothy 4:12 for emphasis, and compare Paul's advice to Timothy with the advice the groups telegraphed to the young preacher.

Suggest that Timothy's example allowed him to lead others to Jesus. Emphasize that the world needs leaders for Jesus and not followers of the world.

Step 3

Arrange the class in a circle and ask students to think of a time they wanted to do something but were told they were "too young." Perhaps they proved that they were not too young. How did they accomplish that task? What could they have done to show that they could do whatever they wanted to do? This is a good time for you to share your own experience.

Tell the class that many older people feel that young people today do not behave as they should. They read newspaper stories about young people who are involved in gangs or commit crimes. They may hear young people use bad language and see some behave rudely or crudely, so they feel all young people are bad. Ask, "How can you demonstrate that you are God's leaders in spite of your age?" Write the answers on a poster board and post it as a reminder to the class.

Suggest that the only way we can be sure of our example is to ask for God's help. Join hands in prayer. Perhaps each student could ask for God's help specifically for one of the ideas listed on the poster.

Materials
poster board, marker

Take It to the Next Level

Tell the students that a special visitor has a challenge for each of them. Leave the room (or simply turn your back) and return dressed in a trench coat, hat, and dark glasses carrying a briefcase. Introduce yourself as an agent of the CIA. Explain that CIA stands for "Christ In Action" and that you have a mission for each of them. Take a tape recorder out of your briefcase and play the following prerecorded message: "Greetings from CIA headquarters. Welcome to the CIA Secret Service. As you know, there is much evil in the world, and that evil can only be blotted out by good. Your mission, should you choose to accept it, is to blot out evil by doing one secret service each day and recording the results in your Secret Service Journal.

"Remember, the service must be done secretly or, if not secretly, then unselfishly and without the other person expecting it. You will have the complete support of the Commander-in-Chief Himself. Please report your success to your group each week. This message will self destruct in ten seconds."

Materials
overcoat, hat, dark glasses, briefcase, tape recorder, pre-recorded tape with message, photocopies of pages 70–72

Leader or Follower?

Return without your costume and give the students photocopies of the journal cover and sheets from pages 70 and 71 that you have prepared. The journal should include enough pages for four weeks (fourteen pages for student). Also include a photocopy of page 72 to suggest ways in which they can secretly serve. Assure the students that these are only suggestions. Their own ideas will probably be much better!

Close with prayer.

CIA SECRET SERVICE JOURNAL

AGENT _____

CIA SECRET SERVICE JOURNAL

DATE:

SERVICE RENDERED:

RESULTS:

DATE:

SERVICE RENDERED:

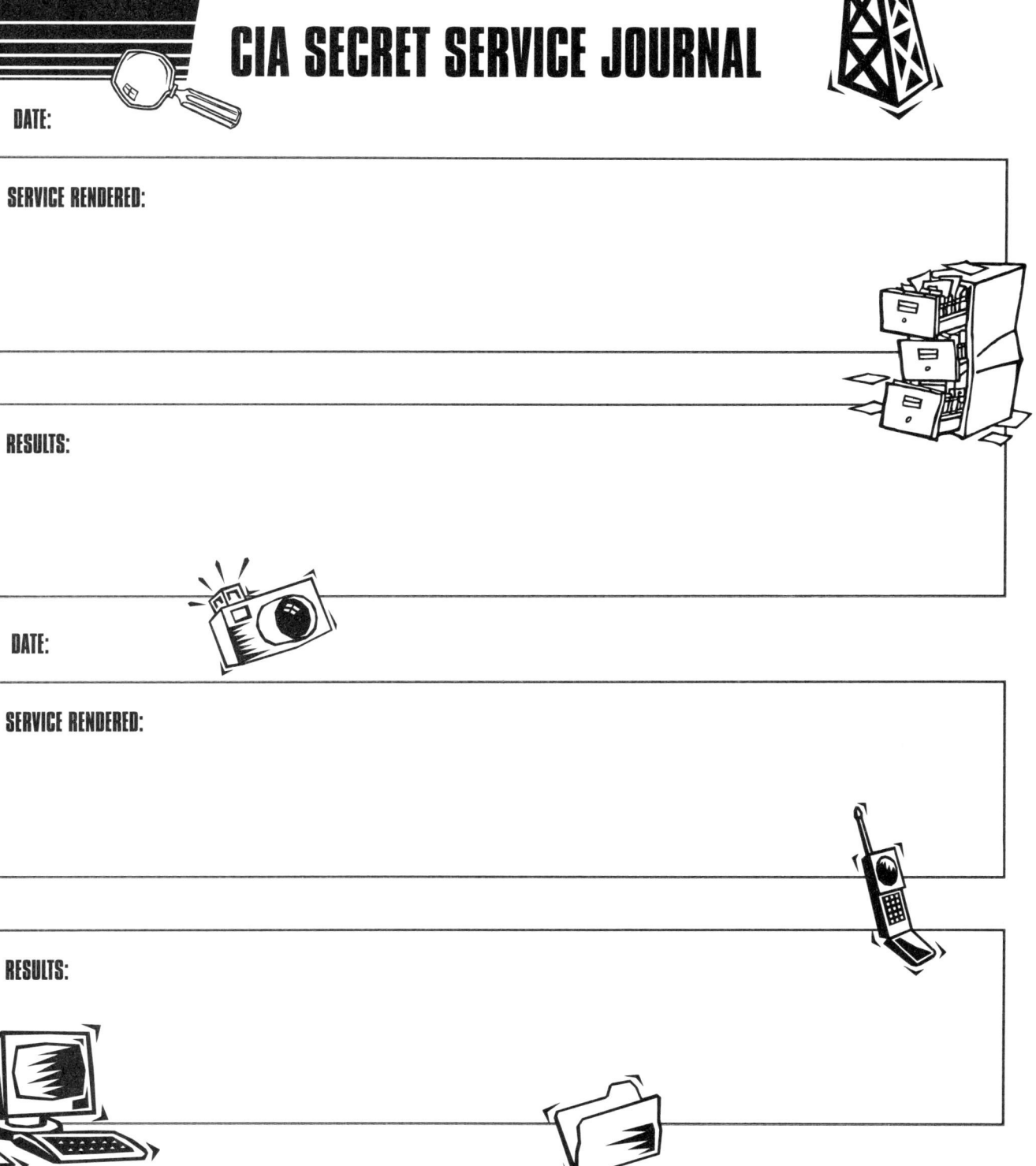

RESULTS:

SECRET SERVICE IDEAS

(Note: Some service ideas may be things you do, not secretly, but unselfishly and without the other person expecting it.)

1. Take out the trash without anyone knowing it.
2. Ask the classmate who always is alone to sit with you and your friends at lunch.
3. Write a note to a teacher telling him that you appreciate his hard work. (Be sure to disguise your handwriting.)
4. Polish your Dad or Mom's shoes after they have gone to bed.
5. Leave a flower in the kitchen or beside your Mom's bed.
6. Pick up toys for your little brother or sister.
7. Mow an older neighbor's lawn or rake leaves when they are away from home.
8. Buy your best friend her favorite candy bar and slip it into her desk or book bag.
9. Empty the dishwasher when no one is looking.
10. Send a card to a shut-in.
11. Water the house plants.
12. Give your pet a bath.
13. Slip a note of congratulations into a friend's book when he makes a good grade or does a report.
14. Wash the family car.
15. Clean the bathtub.
16. Clean your room (or your brother's or sister's room).
17. Write a special letter to your grandmother.
18. Help a younger child with her homework or listen to her read.
19. Leave a batch of cookies (or some doughnuts) for a friend or neighbor.
20. Give something you own to someone who needs it.

Session 2

Needs, Wants, or Stuff?

Scripture: 1 Timothy 6:10

Know the difference between wants and needs.
Feel a need for spiritual gifts instead of earthly things.
Commit personal resources to God.

Get Into the Game

Arrange the chairs in a circle and distribute paper and markers or pens. Have students fold their papers into four equal parts. Ask students to think about the things that belong to them, as opposed to family possessions. Give them a couple of minutes to think. Then set the following scenario:

Your family has learned from the local weather authorities that your home may be in the path of a hurricane (or tornado, flood, or forest fire), and you must evacuate immediately. You can, however, take a few possessions. Your parents give you ten minutes to choose four items to take. Using the sheet of paper, draw four things that you would choose.

After students have sketched their selections, ask them to prioritize them by numbering the squares from one to four. Then ask the students to share their first choice and briefly tell why they made that selection. Teachers should also complete the activity and be willing to share their first choices.

Conclude the activity with another weather bulletin. Inform the class that their homes were spared from disaster, and they may return home and put their possessions back into place. At this point, have each student fold his paper and put it away in a pocket, purse, or Bible.

Materials
paper, pens or markers

Step 1

Begin this session by writing the following three words on the chalkboard: needs, wants, stuff. Ask the students to help you define each of the words. If you prefer, have the definitions already written out. Then you can ask the students if they agree with the definitions, or if they would change them in any way.

Materials
chalkboard and chalk, poster board, markers, magazines and newspapers, scissors, glue.

Use the following definitions:

Needs—something you must have; a necessity.

Wants—something you think you need, but can do without.

Stuff—things you may want that are of questionable value.

Divide the class into groups, giving each a poster board and markers. Have them divide the poster board into three columns, labeled "Needs," "Wants," and "Stuff." Then, using catalogues or newspaper ads, have the groups cut and paste pictures of items under the appropriate labels.

You may prefer to divide the class into three groups and assign one category to each group. That group would then write the label and definition on its poster board and find pictures to illustrate that label.

After the groups have finished working, have each group choose one item (or more, if time allows) from each category and tell why they labeled it as a need, a want, or stuff.

If time allows, have students take out their sketches of the four items they chose to save and decide if that item is a want, a need, or just stuff. Let them do this privately, without any judgments from the teacher or other students.

Step 2

Tell the students that the needs they have been dealing with are all things that we can touch, taste, see, or smell, such as food, clothing, and shelter. These are "material things," and they come to us through God's blessings. However, some necessities we may not be able to touch, taste, see, or smell. These also come to us through God's blessings. These we call "spiritual gifts."

Using the same groups as before, ask each group to use their Bibles to make a list of at least ten spiritual needs that we each have. Provide the following Scriptures by writing them on a poster board, on the chalkboard, or on a hand-out for each group. Encourage the students to use their Bible study skills to find additional Scriptures that indicate a need that God supplies.

John 3:16 (Jesus, eternal life, salvation)

Romans 5:5 (love of God)

Luke 1:77, 78 (salvation, forgiveness of sins)

Luke 18: 29, 30 (eternal life)

Philippians 3:20 (Heaven)

John 8:31, 32 (truth)

Romans 5:17 (grace)

Galatians 5:22, 23 (love, joy, peace, patience, kindness, goodness, faithfulness, gentleness, self control)

Materials
poster board or chalkboard, Bibles, pens and markers

Step 3

After the groups have finished, let them share their lists. Then ask, "How can we acquire God's gifts? Can we buy them? Trade for them? Earn them?"

Next have them read Matthew 7:7, 8 and 1 Timothy 6:10. Contrast the two verses. Ask if the love of money leads to spiritual gifts or perhaps just to more stuff.

Conclude with prayers in which each group specifically asks God for the needs on its list.

Materials
Bibles

Take It to the Next Level

Call a special meeting of the "CIA Agents." (You could wear the coat, hat, and dark glasses again, if you wish.) Ask for reports on the previous week's activities. Allow the Agents to tell at least one secret service they performed. Ask questions of each agent so the group sees the consequences of the service (cleaning out the bathtub gave Mom an extra thirty minutes to read her favorite magazine; inviting a loner to eat lunch has resulted in a new friendship). Remember, teachers are also special agents and need to report. This not only provides a positive model for students, but gives teachers an opportunity to help students link consequences with behavior.

After the sharing session, tell the agents that you have received a coded message from CIA Headquarters. Have it written on a transparency, or a piece of poster board and ask them to help you decipher it:

Materials
disguise from last lesson, transparency or poster board with message written on it, marker, photocopies of page 77, pens or pencils

T H I S   W E E K   U S E   M O N E Y

20 8 9 19   23 5 5 11   21 19 5   13 15 14 5 25

When the students have deciphered the message, ask them to tell you what they think it means. Lead them to the conclusion that since God provides for most of our material needs and wants by allowing us to have the money we need to purchase those items, one way we can use our spiritual gifts is by sharing that money with others.

Tell students, "As secret agents, CIA Headquarters wants us to use some of our money this week to serve someone else." Ask for ideas, emphasizing that the amount does not have to be large to be significant. *(Send a contribution to charity, pay for a telephone call to one of God's workers in another city or country, give more than usual in the church contribution, take a little brother or sister for a special treat, rent a children's video for a busy mom and watch it with her small children while she takes a nap or runs an errand, give to a homeless person).*

Distribute photocopies of page 77. The "Budget Audit and Analysis" can help determine how much money they can use for their "secret service." (Note: If you have a student in the class who may not have any money of his own, help him understand that God does not expect us to give what we do not have. Help him find another way to serve this week.)

Close with a special prayer thanking God for meeting our needs and for granting us our wants. Ask him to help us to make good decisions with our money and to guide the class as they perform their secret services in the coming week.

Budget Audit and Analysis

Property of _____

	Last Week	This Week

Income
    Allowance
    Additional Earnings
    Other:
Total Income		

Expenses:
(Please itemize)
    Needs
    Wants
    Stuff
    Other
      Contributions
      Gifts
      Savings
Total Expenses		

Based on this audit, last week, I

Based on this analysis, this week, I will

Session 3

Time: A Commodity or a Resource?

Scripture: Ephesians 5:15, 16

Analyze use of personal time.
Examine time from God's perspective.
Commit weekly time for God.

Get Into the Game

Americans are very conscious about time. Since you will ask the question today whether we use time as a commodity or a resource, begin the session in a creative way that will focus the students' attention on time. Choose one of the following suggestions or develop your own:

1. Hide an alarm clock (or clocks) in the room and set it to go off just after the class begins. Give a prize to the person or team that locates the clock and turns off the alarm. Talk briefly about alarms and why we need them.

2. Play a video clip of the White Rabbit in *Alice in Wonderland* with his large watch and his, "I'm late! I'm late!" speech. Ask students to share a time when they were late.

3. Bring in as many examples of time pieces that you can find (wind up clock, clock radio, wrist watch, pocket watch, digital clock, hour glass, mantle clock, sun dial). Have students give one advantage and one disadvantage of each instrument.

4. Write the numbers 1–90 on the board. Ask students to close their eyes and open them when they believe that 90 seconds has elapsed. Keep time by touching the numbers in second increments. Have the students write down or remember what number you were pointing to when they opened their eyes. You will probably want to do this at least twice. Ask for student reactions as to whether they were fast, slow, or on time.

5. Select a country in which your church has a missionary and use a time zone map (try the telephone directory) to determine the actual time in that county and decide what the missionary might be doing while you are in Bible class, such as sleeping, visiting church members, or eating lunch.

Materials
alarm clocks, TV and VCR, video clip of *Alice in Wonderland,* various clocks and time pieces, chalk and chalkboard, time zone map or chart

After the motivational activity, read Ephesians 5:15, 16 and discuss what it means when the writer says "make the most of your time."

Step 1

Divide the class into groups of four or five. Give them a photocopy of page 82 entitled, "What Can We Say About Time?" Tell the students that you want them to write down sayings about time or ways we describe or use time. Start them off with one or two already listed on the hand-out. Prepare a list ahead of time so that you can circulate among the groups to give suggestions if the students run out of ideas. Your list might include the following: buy time, give time, use time, save time, waste time, spend time, a stitch in time saves nine, time heals all wounds, running out of time, quality time, time on task, making time, borrowed time.

After the groups have completed their lists, have each group give the number of phrases on their list. Then, have the group with the shortest list read its list as you write their responses on the board. As the first group reads, the other groups should mark out any phrases on their lists that are duplicates. Then, have the second group add its unduplicated phrases to your list. Continue until all groups have responded.

Ask the students to help you decide if the phrase indicates that time is a commodity (C), a resource (R), or both a commodity and a resource (B). Define a commodity as something that is of use or value, such as an article of trade. Often commodities are easily available and may be taken for granted. Examples of commodities include butter, sugar, grains, and coffee. A resource is something that is used to meet a need, such as oil, gas, coal, or lumber. Both commodities and resources can be used positively or they can be wasted. Go through the list you have complied and mark each saying with a C, R, or B.

When students complete the task, ask them for a generalization about time. Lead them to the conclusion that time is both a commodity and a resource. At this phase of their lives, they have a great deal of time—for them it is both a commodity and a resource. However, it can be used positively or it can be wasted. Refer to the day's Scripture and encourage them to be wise in using their time.

Materials
photocopies of page 82, pens or pencils, chalk and chalkboard

Step 2

After reading the Scripture again, divide the class into pairs. Ask the pairs to list ten ways they can use time wisely (*studying, praying, doing chores, resting*) and ten ways in which they

Materials
Bibles, paper, pens or pencils

use time unwisely (*too much television, making excuses, gossiping, listening to the wrong kind of music*). Have the pairs read their lists and tell what they feel is the wisest use of time and the most unwise use of time.

Now read James 4:14. Discuss the fact that time for all of us is really rather short, but that if we use our time wisely and as a resource for God, He promises us time that goes on forever Next read 1 John 20:31.

Close with a prayer in which you ask God to help students to use time wisely.

Step 3

It is time for another meeting of the CIA Agents. To make this a little more dramatic, produce a note that was mysteriously delivered earlier. The note will inform the agents that their arch enemy known as "S" (for Satan) has discovered their meeting place and has bugged it. They must, therefore, find a safe place to report on the previous week's activities and receive this week's assignment. If an empty room is available, lead the students to that location. Other possibilities include a storage room or a supply closet. Add to the drama by turning out the lights and having the discussion with a flashlight or a candle.

Begin this activity by telling the students how you, as the teacher, used some of your money for God this past week. Emphasize how using your money to help someone else made you feel. Then ask others to share their experiences and their feelings.

Read the last of the message from headquarters, which instructs each agent to plan one secret service this week that involves giving time (*reading to a little brother or sister, babysitting for a young mother without asking for pay, asking parents for a special chore that needs to be done and then giving up TV time to do it, volunteering to help a teacher clean chalkboards or arrange a book shelf.*) Encourage the students to record the results of their gift of time in their Secret Service Journals.

Materials
note prepared in advance, flashlight or candle

Take It to the Next Level

Distribute photocopies of page 83 entitled, "Time Management Study." Ask students to complete it honestly and prayerfully. They are to choose one day this past week to analyze and one day in the coming week to make a plan. Each part of the pie graph equals one hour, for a total of 24 hours. They are to color in the graph according to how they used time on the day they selected from last week and how they plan to use time this

Materials
photocopies of page 83, pens or pencils, crayons or markers

week. They may add other colors and categories to the key if they wish.

Provide a private place for each student to work or use the sheet for a take-home activity. Emphasize that this analysis of how they use their time will be between themselves and God. They need not share it with anyone.

Close with the following prayer: "Father, help us to be careful how we walk. Help us to walk not as unwise men, but as wise, making the most of our time. Amen."

What Can We Say About Time?

1. Save time
2. Waste time
3. _____
4. _____
5. _____
6. _____
7. _____
8. _____
9. _____
10. _____
11. _____
12. _____
13. _____
14. _____
15. _____

Time Management Study

Student's Name

_____

Last Week (Day):

_____

Instructions
Color the chart as follows:

  Red=time asleep
  Blue=time eating
  Yellow=time studying
  Green=time watching TV
  Brown=time wasted

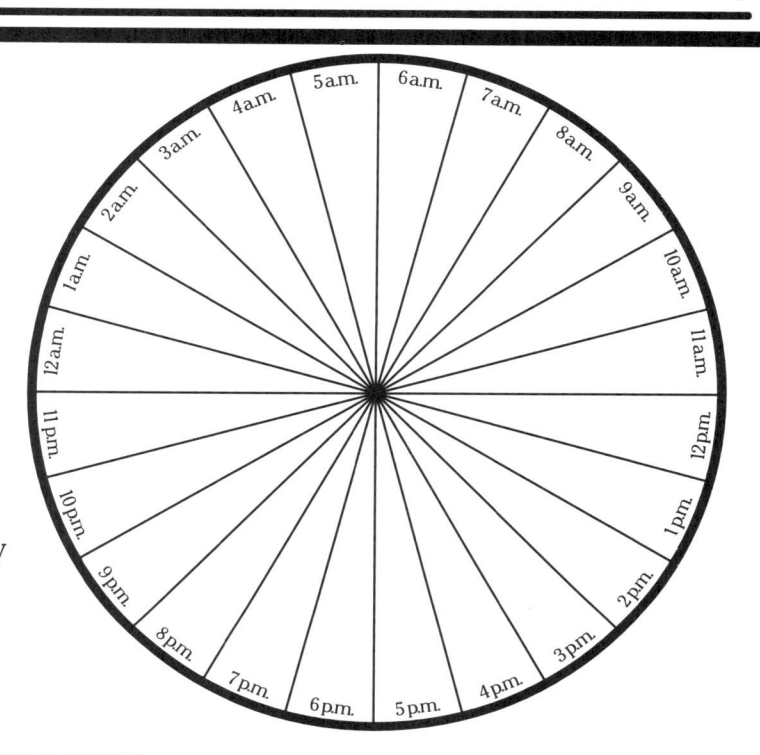

Plan for this week

Day:

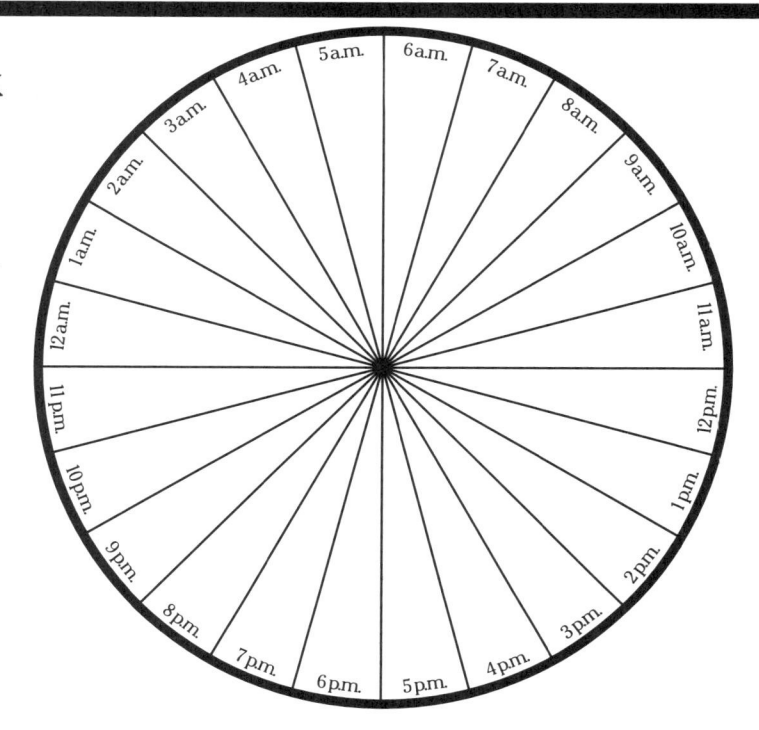

_____

Session 4

A Word Is Worth How Much?

Scripture: James 3:5

Examine the power of words.
Feel the emotional impact of God's Word.
Use words in a positive way.

Get Into the Game

Focus the students' attention on speech by playing "gossip." Arrange the students in a line or a circle. Tell the students that they must listen carefully to the person giving them the message because it cannot be repeated. The person delivering the message needs to speak as clearly as possible. Begin the first game by whispering a sentence that may be difficult for the student to understand, such as "Sam sent several sandwiches to Susan Sunday" or "Barbara brought brownies by for Brady's breakfast." Have the last person in the line say the message aloud and compare it to the original message. You may want to do this several times, ending with a different student each time. Ask students why they feel that the message became garbled.

Suggest that one of the problems may be that the message was not very important to anyone in the group, or that other noises may have interfered with the listening. Show them the listening tube that you prepared before class. (This can be made by covering a cardboard tube from the center of a paper towel roll with contact paper or just labeling it "listening tube.")

Play the game again. This time, one student holds the tube to his ear while the message is repeated clearly into the other end. Use very simple messages such as "God loves you!" "Jesus died for our sins" or "Believe in Jesus!" The tube should carry the message clearly, and the message should reach the other end without being changed.

Suggest that when we speak God's words, the message is clear if it comes from a clear heart that filters out the world, just as the tube filtered out the noises around us.

Materials
cardboard, paper towel tube

Step 1

Read James 3:5 and ask students to give you some illustrations of how the tongue, small as it may be, can do great things. Examples can be negative such as how gossip may hurt someone; or positive, such as the Gettysburg Address, which is very short but powerful.

Divide the class into two groups. The leader of each group will be the person whose birthday is closest. Select one group to be the Plus group and the other the Minus group. Each group is given a stack of index cards. The Plus group is to list as many ways as possible that the tongue can be used in a positive way (*praise, compliment, encourage, sing hymns, bless, pray, teach, preach, comfort*). The Minus group is to list as many ways as possible that the tongue can be used in a negative way (*criticize, put down, curse, hurt, insult, gossip, ridicule, taunt, lie, condemn*). You may want to provide a thesaurus in case the students would like to use it.

After the groups have finished their cards, have the Minus group select and read one of their cards. The Plus group will then try to find one of their cards that is the opposite. For example, if the Minus group calls out *criticize,* the Plus group could counter with *compliment.* After the cards have all been used, discuss how each group felt. Ask, "Was it easier to find positive words or negative words? How do the positive words make you feel? How do the negative words make you feel?"

Another way to teach this activity would be to make several sets of negative and positive word cards before class. Put the students into groups and have them match the negative with the positive. Ask them to be ready to give an example of one of their matches, or to tell why they put them together.

Materials
Bibles, blank index cards, pens or pencils, thesaurus (optional)

Step 2

Divide the students into pairs and give each pair a photocopy of page 87 and one of the positive cards from Step 1. Have the pairs write a dialogue that gives an example of that positive use of speech. If you use this suggestion, have students write James 3:5 in the box for the Scripture.

Or have the students use their Bible study skills to locate a Scripture concerning speech or the tongue, write that Scripture in the box, and then write a dialogue that demonstrates the Scripture application.

Let each pair read or "act out" the dialogue. If time allows, have the participants tell how that particular scenario made them feel about words.

Materials
photocopies of page 87, pens and pencils, positive cards from Step 1, Bibles

Close with a prayer that asks God for help in using positive words as we interact with others.

Step 3

Cut examples from newspapers, magazines, and comic books to show how artists or ad writers emphasize certain words. Some examples might include the headlines of a paper, the word "Boom!" from a comic strip, or words that have illustrations added, such as arranging the word jump over a fence or adding "Zzzzzz" above the word sleep.

Prepare a list entitled "Godly Vocabulary" on a poster board or a chalkboard. This list should include such words as God, Jesus, Christ, love, heart, forgiveness, blessing, praise, Hallelujah, angel, Heaven, hope, grace, joy, peace, goodness, mercy, amen, glory, spirit, holy. Ask each student to select a word and illustrate it using classroom supplies such as construction paper, scissors, markers, crayons, paste, pieces of fabric, or glitter.

When students have finished, place their illustrations on a bulletin board, or display them around the room.

Materials
newspapers, magazines, comic books, chalk and chalkboard or poster board and markers, scissors, construction paper, glue, crayons, pieces of fabric, glitter

Take It to the Next Level

Before class, make photocopies of page 88, fold them, and place them in envelopes—one per student.

Call a meeting of the CIA Secret Agents. Ask if there are any reports from the previous week's activities. Since you, the teacher, are also a secret agent, begin by telling how you gave some of your time this past week and the results of that gift of time. Allow others to report as time permits or as they wish.

Tell them that this week's message from headquarters contains special instructions for each agent. They are to select the envelope with their name on it and keep it confidential. This assignment is so secret that they will not share it next week—it will be only between themselves and the Supreme Leader (God) Himself.

Close with prayer asking God's guidance as we use His gift of language.

Materials
photocopies of page 88, envelopes

"I said... You said..."

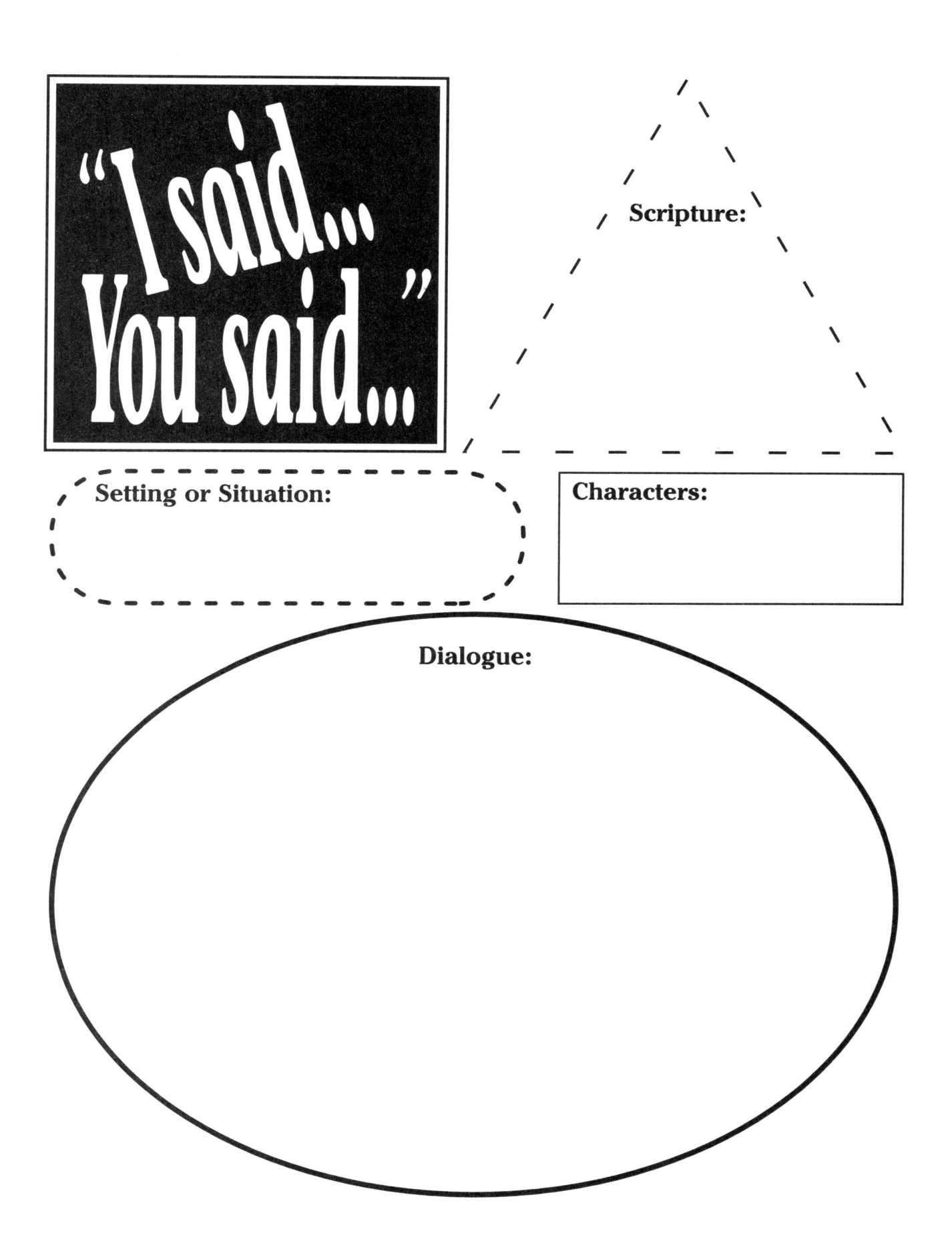

Scripture:

Setting or Situation:

Characters:

Dialogue:

Dear CIA Agent:

Your mission this week is to accomplish the following tasks. You may do them in any order. Make a check when you complete a task. When you have finished all of the assignments, destroy this message.

- ☐ Praise someone for a job well done.

- ☐ Compliment a friend on how he or she looks.

- ☐ Tell a Bible story to a young child, or invite a friend to come to Sunday school.

- ☐ Tell your parents that you love them.

- ☐ Pray a special prayer for someone who may be ill or experiencing problems.

Bridge the Gap

Things I Do... Things You Do

Scripture: Luke 2:49-52

Know that family members may see the same event differently.
Express feelings with family members.
Plan to change a negative behavior.

Get Into the Game

Begin the class in one of the following ways:

1. Before the class begins, videotape a segment from a current television show that shows interaction between parents and children. The situation may involve a problem situation or it may simply be an exchange of ideas, but it needs to be realistic and honest. Preteens are quick to know when they are objects of ridicule or when they are presented in a way that makes them seem immature or as poor decision makers. On the other hand, many television shows portray parents as inept and children as being wise and hip. Therefore, choose an episode that does not reflect unfairly on either the child or parent. Give each family member a "critique card" that asks for the following information: *Who was involved? What was the main idea of the episode? What sentence would you use to describe the child? What sentence would you use to describe the parent?*

After the critiques are completed, put each family in a group and have them compare answers. The preteen should share his answer to the first question and then the parent. Discuss reasons for differences. Next the parent shares an answer and the preteen follows. After answers have been compared, ask each family to rate their similarities on a scale of one to ten

Materials
TV and VCR, videotape of TV program, index cards with questions written on them, pens or pencils, magazine illustration or poster, guest, paper

89 Things I Do . . .

(ten as highest number of similar answers). Take a survey to see if most families agree or differ in their answers.

2. Select a magazine illustration or a poster for each family group that shows parents and children engaged in some activity. Ask each family member to look at the illustration for a few seconds. Then ask each person to list as many details from the picture as possible. Calculate the same responses and have the groups suggest reasons for differences.

3. Have an outsider come into the classroom and act in a strange manner (steal a purse, shout at the teacher, give a speech) then leave quickly. Ask each family member to write down a description of the outsider. Have parents and preteens compare their answers.

Close this session with a reading of Romans 15:5. Have each family read the verse and then pray together, asking God's help that their family might be of one mind according to Christ Jesus.

Step 1

Begin by distributing photocopies of page 92 and pens or pencils. They are to read the story and then be ready to answer the following questions as a family group. There will, however, be one rule: preteens must answer the questions concerning the parents and parents must answer the questions for the preteens.

Materials
photocopies of page 92, pens or pencils

1. What was the problem? *(The boy Jesus stayed in Jerusalem.)*

2. How did the parents view the situation? Was it a problem for them? Why or why not? *(They were upset with him for staying behind.)*

3. How did the boy see the situation? Was it a problem for him? Why or why not? *(He was following a higher call.)*

4. How did the parents feel as a result of the problem? *(concerned, frightened, astonished)*

5. How did the boy feel? *(calm)*

6. What was the solution or the outcome? *(He was obedient and left with them.)*

Step 2

Have four students prepared a brief synopsis of the last four sessions. Or, you may prefer to do this yourself. The following might help in this activity:

Session 1 asked preteens to decide to be leaders rather than followers. Using Timothy as an example, they learned that they are not too young to lead others by example.

Session 2 looked at how we use our money and asked preteens to examine the difference between needs, wants, and stuff. It encouraged us to look to the spiritual needs that only God can supply.

Session 3 helped preteens look at their use of time and whether that time was used wisely, as we might use a resource.

Session 4 looked at the power of words and their impact on our behavior and our example.

Discuss the fact that many problems that arise between parents and preteens center around these topics: example, money, time, and vocabulary. Many of these problems may be because parents and preteens do not always see things the same way, as demonstrated in the Get Into the Game activity. The purpose of the next task is to help preteens and parents better understand each other.

Step 3

Give each parent and preteen a Plus and Minus Sheet (photocopies of pages 93 and 94) and ask both to follow the instructions as specific as possible. Each preteen is to make one positive and one negative statement about each of the four areas in regards to themselves, and then concerning their parent or parents. The parents are to do the same for the preteen and then for himself or herself. After the activity, parents and preteens exchange the sheets and discuss the answers. Ask them to respond honestly—without anger and without judgment. Remember, these are perceptions but true or not, perceptions interfere with communication.

Materials
photocopies of page 93 and 94, pens or pencils

Take It to the Next Level

After comparing the lists, ask each family member to tell one new thing they have learned about the other member. Distribute photocopies of page 95 and have everyone cut out and fill in the Pledge Card. You might suggest that the family make a plan to change one negative item that appears on both lists into a positive action, or to make a list of two or three ways that the parent or preteen might modify their behavior.

Close with a family prayer time in which each group asks God to help them better understand each other and work together to be of one mind in Him.

Materials
photocopies of page 95, pens or pencils, scissors

Conflict Resolution

Read Luke 2:41-52 then answer the questions.

1. What was the problem?

2. How did the parents view the situation? Was it a problem for them? Why or why not?

3. How did the boy see the situation? Was it a problem for him? Why or why not?

4. How did the parents feel as a result of the problem?

5. How did the boy feel?

6. What was the solution or the outcome?

Pluses and Minuses
for the Parent

Leader or Follower
One positive thing my preteen feels that I do in being an example is

One negative thing my preteen feels that I do in being an example is

One positive thing I feel my preteen does in being an example is

One negative thing I feel my preteen does in being an example is

Time
One positive way my preteen feels that I use time is

One negative way my preteen feels that I use time is

One positive way I feel that my preteen uses time is

One negative way I feel that my preteen uses time is

Money
One positive way my preteen feels that I use money is

One negative way my preteen feels that I use money is

One positive way I feel that my preteen uses money is

One negative way I feel that my preteen uses money is

Language
One positive way my preteen feels that I use language is

One negative way my preteen feels that I use language is

One positive way I feel that my preteen uses language is

One negative way I feel that my preteen uses language is

©1997 by The Standard Publishing Company. Permission is granted to reproduce this page for ministry purposes only—not for resale.

Pluses and Minuses
for the Preteen

Leader or Follower
One positive thing my parent(s) feels that I do in being an example is

One negative thing my parent(s) feels that I do in being an example is

One positive thing I feel my parent(s) does in being an example is

One negative thing I feel my parent(s) does in being an example is

Time
One positive way my parent(s) feels that I use time is

One negative way my parent(s) feels that I use time is

One positive way I feel that my parent(s) uses time is

One negative way I feel that my parent(s) uses time is

Money
One positive way my parent(s) feels that I use money is

One negative way my parent(s) feels that I use money is

One positive way I feel that my parent(s) uses money is

One negative way I feel that my parent(s) uses money is

Language
One positive way my parent(s) feels that I use language is

One negative way my parent(s) feels that I use language is

One positive way I feel that my parent(s) uses language is

One negative way I feel that my parent(s) uses language is

FOLD LINE

Pledge Card

I _____ pledge to help my family be of one mind in Jesus Christ by _____

_____.

I further pledge to ask God's help in changing my behavior by going to Him in prayer about my pledge each day.

Signature _____

Date _____

Go to Extremes

Leaders Become Servants

Scripture: John 13:4-17

Know Jesus as a servant.
Feel the satisfaction of serving.
Become a willing servant.

Get Into the Game

Use John 13:4-17 as the script for a short drama. As the teacher, you may wish to play the part of Jesus and have an assistant or a student play Peter. The rest of the class can be the other apostles. Costumes are not necessary, but they will add to the effect. They need not be elaborate. For example, Jesus could have a robe that could be removed. Strips of cloth or towels and robe could become head coverings for Peter and the apostles. As you act out the Scripture, say Jesus' exact words. You may want to do the drama several times if other students wish to be Peter or Jesus.

Talk about Jesus as a leader. Not only did the twelve follow Him, but others wanted to make Him a king. Emphasize the fact that Jesus knew He would die soon, and the apostles would become the leaders who would spread His message throughout the world. He wanted them to know that great leaders are, first of all, great servants.

Materials
costumes and props (water, basin, towel)

Step 1

Begin this activity by talking about the class as CIA (Christ in Action) agents. Report that they worked alone and did many good things with their leadership, time, money, and words. Ask

Materials
poster board or newsprint, markers

96   Leaders Become Servants

them what they could have done if they had been able to multiply themselves by five or ten or twenty (the number in your class). Have them suggest things that they could have done if they had all worked together on one project. Write the suggestions on a poster board or on a strip of newsprint.

After the suggestions are made, tell the class that the group will vote on one of the ideas as a servant project. Have each student go to the poster board and mark his or her choice. The suggestion with the highest number of votes will be the class project.

Remind the class of Jesus' promise to bless those who become servants. Then offer a prayer that God will bestow that blessing on each of them as they work together to become the kind of servants that Jesus wants His leaders to be.

Step 2

Distribute photocopies of page 98, and as a class, plan the project using the model given. The teacher might put the plan on a transparency and then allow each student to fill out his own paper as the plan is made.

Materials
photocopies of page 98, overhead projector and transparency, pens or pencils, marker

Step 3

Carry out the project. You might begin by reading John 13:17 and then once again pray for God's help and His blessing.

Materials
Bibles

Take It to the Next Level

After the project is completed, photocopy the evaluation form on page 99 and use it with the class so that they can reflect on the project and how it made them feel as they worked together to become servant leaders.

Close with the song, "Make Me a Servant."

Materials
photocopies of page 99, pens or pencils

Planning for Servanthood

Project: _____
_____

Purpose: _____
_____

Materials Needed: _____
_____

Possible Problems or Obstacles	How to Overcome

Step by Step Planning	Time Table	Person(s) Responsible

Evaluation

Project: _____
_____

Was project completed? _____
_____

Were there obstacles? How were they overcome? _____
_____

Did the plan have to be changed? If so, why and how? _____
_____

What were the results? _____
_____

How did this project make you feel? _____
_____

(Before it began)   (During the project)   (After completion)

What lessons were learned from this activity? _____
_____

What does it mean to be a servant? _____
_____

Unit 3

World-Changing Power

When I was ten, the word "missionary" evoked a mental picture of an odd person in a remote country eating bugs and worms.

Ironically, I grew up on a mission field and was the daughter of a missionary. My father was the director of a church-planting mission in New York. My family lived on mission support. For some reason I did not connect my life to the concept of a "missionary." My own life seemed very "normal."

Preteens struggle with identity. They desire to belong and fit in with their peers. To be "different" is to be an outcast, a social pariah.

It is important to stress to preteens that God has called normal people to do normal things. Christians are missionaries. We are the "salt" and "light" in our world. Our daily walk with Christ, and the deeds of kindness we do to meet the needs of others, are all part of the mission work God has given us.

God didn't call us to be something we are not. He did not say "strive to become salt and light." He said we are salt and light.

As we live for Christ, we will shine in our world. These sessions are written to help your students understand their unique and important roles as a missionary in their world. Your preteens will begin to see God's desire for their lives; to shine as lights in their world for Christ, not to hide what is natural for a Christian.

Session 1
Know that God has sent missionaries into the world to bring people to a knowledge of Him.
Feel gratitude that Jesus came as a missionary so that we might know God.
Express thanks to God for sending Jesus.

Session 2
Know God wants us to be "salt" and "light" in the world.
Feel the desire to introduce one friend to Jesus through a "salt" or "light" deed.
Commit to do one "salt" or "light" deed for that friend in the coming week.

Session 3
Know that each member of the body of Christ (the church) plays an important part in bringing others to God through Christ.
Feel they are essential contributors to the mission as missionaries and as supporters to other missionaries
Pray for one church missionary daily for one week.

Session 4
Know there are missionaries all over the world who need their support.
Feel a desire to assist and encourage these missionaries.
Write a letter of encouragement to one missionary.

In addition, this unit will help open the eyes of these students to understand the needs of others in the "body of Christ," the church, who have chosen other mission fields.

Ultimately, they will be provided exciting opportunities to get involved in both their mission field and in the lives of other missionaries.

Unit Projects

Mission Information Center
Gather information about the missions your church supports. Create a colorful display area with photos and letters from the missionaries. Gather cultural artifacts to display for missionaries in foreign lands.

Invite a Missionary
Contact a local benevolence organization and invite a representative to talk to the students about the work of that mission.

Letter Station and Photo Booth
Set up a station in the room with photos of missionary kids. Include an address, a brief description, and a prayer need of the missionary kids. Have note cards and envelopes for the students to correspond with missionary children. Have an instant-photo camera available for your students to take pictures of themselves and send with the notes.

Teen Missions International, Inc.
885 East Hall Road
Merritt Island, FL 32953-8443
Phone (407) 453-0350   Fax (407) 452-7988

This organization sends teens and preteens on mission trips. Upon request, they will send a brochure and a video tape of their program. Both are educational resources regarding missions in the U.S. and abroad. The video shows how children age ten to thirteen can get involved in missionary work.

Daily Devotions

Jesus calls us to be salt and light in our world. Through our caring and meeting the needs of those around us, Christ is seen in us. Being a missionary is not some vocation we choose. It is daily living, breathing, and acting as Christ would. We choose our mission field, not our mission.

You have chosen a wonderful and challenging mission field—your class room. Your commitment to Christ and your daily walk with Him will be the most important part of the sessions you teach. The following is recommended as a daily part of your prayer time as you prepare these sessions.

Pray for:

	Week 1	**Week 2**	**Week 3**	**Week 4**
Monday Yourself	1 John 4:9	Matthew 5:16	Ephesians 4:16	Mark 16:15
Tuesday Your students	2 Corinthians 2:15	Psalm 97:11, 12	Philippians 4:8	2 Thessalonians 2:19, 20
Wednesday Friends of your students	Ephesians 5:1, 2	Psalm 34:5	1 John 4:7	Matthew 28:20
Thursday Parents of your students	Ephesians 6:10	Psalm 18:28	Philippians 4:4, 5	Ephesians 3:16
Friday Missions	3 John 8	Matthew 5:13	Ephesians 6:19	Colossians 1:9
Saturday Other youth leaders	Philippians 3:17	1 Thessalonians 3:12, 13	1 Corinthians 12:27	Philippians 4:6, 7
Sunday Your time with students	1 Thessalonians 2:8	Proverbs 2:4, 5	2 Peter 3:18	1 Corinthians 9:22

Session 1

Mission Possible

Memory Verse: 1 John 4:9
Scriptures: Matthew 10:6-8; 25:35-38; John 3:17; Acts 13:2-4; Romans 5:10; Galatians 4:4

Know that God has sent missionaries into the world to bring people to a knowledge of Him.
Feel gratitude that Jesus came as a missionary so that we might know God.
Express thanks to God for sending Jesus.

Get Into the Game

Cover a wall (4' x 8' or larger depending on the size of your group) with a sheet of butcher paper or bulletin board paper. As the students arrive, have them stand at the wall and draw a picture of a missionary. (Depending on what the kids have been exposed to, they may draw anything from a person in the jungle to an "ordinary" person in a common setting.) After a few minutes have the students explain their drawings.

Ask the students, "What is the mission of the following organizations or people?"
1. The NBA *(to oversee and regulate basketball)*
2. The Ford Co. *(to build cars)*
3. Kellogg *(to make cereal)*
4. NASA *(to explore space)*
5. A missionary *(allow the kids discussion time)*

Say, "Today we will explore the following three questions: What is a missionary? What is the mission of a missionary? How is that mission accomplished?"

Materials
butcher paper or bulletin board paper, tape, markers

Step 1

Activity #1

Before class, tape the following message on a cassette tape. (You may have another person record the message so that the students won't recognize the voice.)

"Good morning. Recently a person approached this class claiming to be a missionary and asking for funds to support the mission effort. To determine whether this is a legitimate request, we need to investigate the validity of this person's claim to be a missionary. Your mission, if you choose to accept

Materials
audio cassette recorder and blank cassette, Bibles, pencils, paper, poster board, and markers

it, is to find a definition for the word, *missionary.* Those working with you have been carefully selected to help you accomplish your mission. Your leader has been given explicit instruction, to aid you in your mission."

Have the students play the recorded message.
On the poster board, make the following chart:

Scripture	**Who?**	**Where?**	**Why?**
1 John 4:9			
Matthew 10:5–8			
Acts 13:2–4			

Have the students look up the Scriptures and write the answers to the questions on the chart.

1. 1 John 4:9. God sent Jesus into the world that we might live through Him. God sent a message of forgiveness and eternal life. Jesus was not only the messenger, but the means for us to come back to God.

2. Matthew 10:5-8. Jesus sent out twelve disciples to the Gentiles to preach the message that God's kingdom had come to earth.

3. Acts 13:2-4. The church sent Paul and Barnabas to Cyprus to do the work of the Holy Spirit. This "work" was to tell people about Jesus and bring them back to God.

Say, "Whenever God had a message, He sent a messenger to deliver it. A missionary is one who is sent from God to a specific place for a special purpose."

Activity #2

Before class, tape the following message. (You may have another person record the message so that the students won't recognize the voice.) Have the students play the recorded message to explain the activity.

"A young person has approached this class desiring to do mission work. He has volunteered his time and resources to do whatever it takes to accomplish the task of a missionary. Your assignment, if you choose to accept it, is to define the mission of a missionary. Those working with you have been carefully selected to help you accomplish your goal. Your leader has been given explicit instructions to aid you in your objective."

Distribute photocopies of page 107 and pencils. Have students fill in the blanks. The answer:
The mission of a missionary is to bring God's message so

Materials
audio cassette recorder and blank cassette, Bibles, pencils, paper, poster board and markers, scissors, photocopies of page 107

that . . . *the world might be saved through his Son.*

Discuss the meaning of each Scripture with the students.

1. Romans 5:10—Our sin has separated us from God. Jesus became a "bridge" to bring us back to God by taking our sin away.

2. Galatians 4:4—Jesus was sent by God to bring us back to Him. Now through Jesus we can be "sons and daughters" of God.

3. 1 John 4:9—Because God loved us, He sent Jesus to give us eternal life though Him.

4. John 3:17—God sent Jesus into the world to save the world.

Activity #3

The mission of this group is to determine how God's mission is accomplished. Read Matthew 25:34-40 aloud together. Have the students write a modern skit using these verses. One narrator can read while the rest of the students act out the story, or they can write specific lines for characters.

Encourage the students to consider "modernizing" the verses by incorporating people with handicaps and unpopular kids at school ("I was a stranger"), people in hospitals or nursing homes ("I was sick"), homeless ("I was hungry"), etc.

Have some students portray the "needy" while others portray the helpers who meet the need.

Prepare the skit to be presented to the entire class in Step 2.

Materials
props such as a can of food, glass of water, Bible, books, or clothes

Step 2

Begin by asking the students, "Does anyone know a missionary? Where does he live? What does he do?" Have students who participated in Activity #1 present their chart. Say, "A missionary is a person who is sent by God to a specific place for a special purpose." Have the students who participated in Activity #2 tell what the mission is. Say, "This mission is to bring people to God though Christ." Have the kids who participated in Activity #3 present their skit. Say, "We accomplish this mission by showing people Christ's love by meeting their needs.

"In light of what you have heard, how many missionaries do we have in this room? We have all been sent by God to a specific place *(our homes, schools, neighborhoods)* for a special purpose *(to bring people back to God through Christ)."*

Step 3

Begin by reading the following story.

"One day, a young girl went swimming at the beach. There was a strong current that day. Without anyone noticing, the

Materials
construction or colored paper, scissors, envelopes, pens, phone book, church directory, stamps, colored pencils or markers

Mission Possible

current began pulling her farther into the ocean. She looked back toward the beach, realized she had been pulled far out in the ocean, and began swimming back to the shore. The current kept pulling her farther and farther away. Panic set in! She could not swim back to safety. The current was just too strong. About this time, a neighbor saw her struggling and swam out to where she was. He was strong. He helped pull her toward the safety of the beach. He saved her life.

Say, "God saw the world was getting farther and farther away from Him. He sent Jesus to rescue us and pull us back to safety. Jesus was a missionary, sent from God to bring us back to God.

"Someone who cared about you told you about Jesus. Who was that person?" Ask each student to share who told them about Jesus. Then say, "That person was a missionary. He obeyed God, and because of his love for God and for you, he told you about Jesus. Let's make a "thank you" note to the person who told you about Jesus." Provide paper, envelopes, phone books, and church directories for the students to look up addresses.

Take It to the Next Level

Have the students write the memory verse (1 John 4:9) on a large index card. Have them write it again, underneath, substituting their name for "us" and "we." On the other side of the card, have them write down two reasons why they are thankful God sent Jesus to be a missionary to them. Give each student a string and seven pieces of Life Savers candy.

Say, "Without Jesus in our lives, we were lost. I want you to commit yourself to thank God each day for loving you enough to send someone to you to tell you about Jesus. Put seven pieces of Life Savers candy on the string. Tie the ends together to make a circle. Take this home. Each time you read your memory verse and thank God for sending Jesus as a life saver, you can eat one. How long will it take you to finish the candy on the string?"

Materials
large index card (4" x 6"), pen or pencil, Life Savers candy, string

What's the Mission?

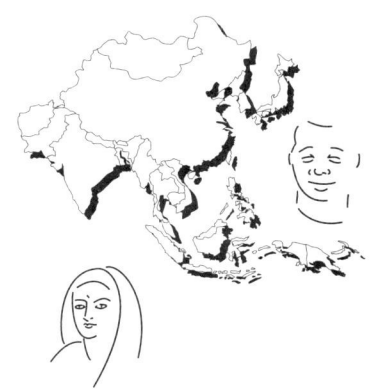

Look up the following Scriptures, then fill in the missing blanks. Put the words in proper order to discover the mission of the missionary. Use the *New International Version*.

Romans 5:10   "having been reconciled, shall we __ __ through his life!"
                                                               4   5

Galatians 4:4   "God sent __ __ . . ."
                                          7   8

1 John 4:9   "He sent His one and only Son into __ __
                                                                             1   2
that we __ live through him."
                  3

John 3:17   "but to save the world __ him."
                                                    6

The mission of a missionary is to bring God's message so that . . .

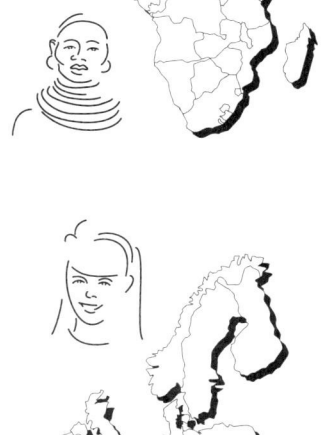

___ ___ ___ ___ ___ ___ ___ ___
 1   2   3   4   5   6   7   8

107   ©1997 by The Standard Publishing Company. Permission is granted to reproduce this page for ministry purposes only—not for resale.

Session 2

Salt and Light

Scriptures: Matthew 5:13—16; Mark 9:50; Colossians 4:6
Memory Verse: Matthew 5:16

Know God wants us to be "salt" and "light" in the world.
Feel the desire to introduce one friend to Jesus through a "salt" or "light" deed.
Commit to do one "salt" or "light" deed for that friend in the coming week.

Get Into the Game

Before the students arrive, hide pennies around the room. Give the students two to three minutes to find as many pennies as they can.

Put two one-dollar bills on the table. Ask the students, "If you had to go to the store right now and needed two dollars, would you rather pick up these bills on the table or find two hundred pennies around the room?" They will probably say they would opt for the dollar bills.

Say, "Jesus said we are to be the light of the world. He said not to hide that light—like I hid the pennies. Our relationship with Jesus affects our lives through our words and actions. When our friends see our loving actions and kind words, they see Jesus in us. Our example is obvious to a searching world, just as the dollar bills are obvious to a person looking for money."

Materials
pennies, two one-dollar bills

Step 1

Activity #1

Have students read Matthew 5:13. Then distribute pens and photocopies of page 112. Say, "For every quality of salt, think of a parallel quality that Christians should have."

Allow students to fill out their pages. Some possible responses follow:

1. Salt adds flavor—Christians use their various God-given gifts to enrich the world.

2. Salt detects wounds—When Christians live the abundant life, others may recognize that something is missing in their own lives.

Materials
Bibles, pens or pencils, photocopies of page 112

Salt and Light

3. Salt's color represents purity—We should lead lives without moral impurities.

4. Salt preserves freshness—Christian influence can keep evil from totally destroying society.

Activity #2

Read Matthew 5:14-16. Give everyone a black crayon and a piece of paper. Ask them to draw a rainbow. Obviously they cannot. Allow the light to reflect through the prism, creating a rainbow. Explain that all color is light refracted. Without light, there is no color.

Have the students close their eyes as you turn out the lights to the room. Without looking have them draw what you describe:

1. a tree, a bird in the tree.
2. a slice of pizza with pepperoni and mushrooms.
3. a house with 2 windows, a door, and a chimney with smoke coming out of the chimney.

Turn on the lights, and have the kids share their pictures. Now have the students draw the same things with light. Tape the signs to the wall. Hang the pictures under the two signs "without light" (hang all the pictures drawn with the eyes closed) and "with light" (hang all the pictures drawn with the eyes opened).

Ask the students, "What are some of the important things light does?" *(Gives us color, allows us to use our eyes, grow plants, etc.)*

Materials

white paper, black or brown crayons for each student, prism, two signs one reading "with light" one reading "without light," tape

Activity #3

Read Matthew 5:16 then ask, "What good deed could you do in your homes, neighborhood, or at school that would make people praise God?" Allow time for response *(mowing an elderly neighbor's lawn, helping someone with homework, etc.)*. When we do good, we are being a light in our world."

Have each student think of a good deeds motto and make a bumper sticker *("Do what's right–Be a light," "If you're kind, no one will ever mind," "Be real cool, don't cheat in school")*.

Materials

colored markers, 3" x 6" pieces of poster board or adhesive paper

Step 2

Have each group share what they have done. The students involved in Activity #1 can discuss the handouts and the uses for salt. The students involved in Activity #2 share their drawings "with light and without light." Say, "There is a great contrast between life with light and without. We who follow Jesus have light. God asks that we shine that light so that others will come to Him." The students involved in Activity #3 may share their bumper stickers. Say, "Our love for Jesus motivates us to do good. When we do good deeds we allow Jesus to shine in our lives. Our light is a contrast to the darkness of the world. People in the world will see that light. This is what Jesus told us to do."

Step 3

Say to the students, "Isn't it interesting that we are called to be salt and light? Salt and light are such normal things. They aren't religious. Jesus doesn't want us to be *religious;* He wants us to use our lives every day to meet people's needs so that they will come to Him. For example, we can talk to someone who's shy, or say something encouraging to people who are down on themselves."

Distribute photocopies of page 113 and pens or pencils, then say, "Think of an ability you have. This could be playing a musical instrument, being a good reader, or baking cookies. Write down your special ability. Think of a way that you could use your ability to do a salt or light deed for someone you know who does not know Jesus."

Divide the students in groups of three or four. Their mission as a group is to introduce Jesus to someone who does not know Him. The groups should work together using each person's ability. Create a plan to show Jesus' love to someone. For example, one student who likes to bake could bake things for a neighbor with young children; one student who likes to read could offer to take the young children and read a Bible story to give the mother a break; a third student could play the instrument for the kids and teach them a song about Jesus. This would be a light not only to the children, but also to the mother.

Have students share their plans. Then say, "God has given out a wide variety of skills and talents to accomplish His mission. We shine individually as a light in the world, and we can shine together as we work in the church to shine for Jesus."

Materials
photocopies of page 113, pens or pencils

Take It to the Next Level

Begin popping the popcorn. Say, "Jesus came as a missionary to us. Someone told us about Jesus." Hold up a kernel of corn. Say, "This is how the world is—how we were—full of potential, but not good for much. But, if we add light, which in this instance comes in the form of heat, the kernel can reach its potential and become something good and nutritious to eat.

"Popcorn is good, but a little tasteless. Salt flavors it quite well and makes it tasty and more appealing. We are the salt of

Materials
popcorn popper, popcorn, salt, paper cups, 4" x 6" index cards, pencils

the earth. We are to do good deeds so that people will see God's goodness and want to know more about Him.

"Jesus was salt and light to the world. His mission was to bring people back to God through Him. Someone told you about Jesus; he or she was a missionary to you. Jesus told us to be salt and light in the world. What good deeds can we do as missionaries in our world?" Allow time for responses.

"Think of one person you know who does not have a relationship with Jesus or does not faithfully attend a church. Think of one thing you can do for this person to make him see God's goodness in you. As we pass the bowl of popcorn around, take a cup for yourself and share with the group one thing you can do this week to be salt and light to one person."

Have the students write the memory verse on one side of the index card (Matthew 5:16). On the other side, have them write the name of a person and deed they will commit to do for that person this week. End in prayer.

Salt Talks

Read Matthew 5:13. Look at the following uses for salt and list some parallel qualities that Christians should have.

Salt Adds Flavor

Salt Detects Wounds

Salt's Color Represents Purity

Salt Preserves Freshness

112 ©1997 by The Standard Publishing Company. Permission is granted to reproduce this page for ministry purposes only—not for resale.

Salt and Light Deeds

My special ability is...

_____
_____
_____
_____
_____

One way I could use this ability to be salt or light for someone is...

_____
_____
_____
_____
_____

Plans for a salt or light deed...

_____
_____
_____
_____
_____

Session 3

Part of the Team

Scriptures: Romans 12:6-8; 1 Corinthians 12:15-17, 21; Ephesians 4:16; 6:19, 20; Philippians 4:14, 16
Memory Verse: 4:16

Know that each member of the body of Christ (the church) plays an important part in bringing others to God through Christ.
Feel they are essential contributors to the mission as missionaries and as supporters to other missionaries
Pray for one church missionary daily for one week.

Get Into the Game

Divide students into groups of five or six. Have them form a circle with their backs to the inside and lock arms at the elbow. Give them the following tasks to do: have them walk across the room, skip across the room, and hop across the room *attached*. The groups that succeed will cooperate and learn to work in unison. Then say, "The Bible says that we are the body of Christ. We are all connected, each with abilities and strengths. When we work together, great things can be accomplished."

Step 1
Activity #1

Divide the students into groups of two or three. Give each group a verse to illustrate: 1 Corinthians 12:15; 12:16; 12:17a; 12:17b; 12:21. For example:

1 Corinthians 12:15—The foot says it does not want to be a part of the body.

1 Corinthians 12:16—This could be a funny cartoon. The ear is walking away from the body saying, "I am not an eye; I do not belong to the body." The body could say, "What? I can't hear you?"

When students have finished their illustrations say, "The Corinthian writer uses humor here to make a point. Our physical bodies would be pretty funny looking if we were only a foot or an eye or a nose. And we would be in deep trouble if our eyes wanted to be feet or our ears wanted to be eyes. The body of Christ is like this too. We are all different. God made us that way, and He wants each of us to use our unique talents for Him."

Materials
paper, pencils, colored markers

Activity #2

Read and discuss Romans 12:6-8 and Ephesians 4:11. Make a poster listing all the gifts mentioned in the Scriptures and define each gift. Have the students write on the poster the name of someone they know in the class or in the church with the gift.

   1. Romans 12:6-8 prophesying (speaking the message of God before God's people), serving, teaching, encouraging, contributing, leadership, mercy.

   2. Ephesians 4:11-13 apostles (witnesses of Christ's resurrection), evangelists (telling people who do not know about the gospel), prophets (speaking the message of God before God's people), pastors (people who shepherd or lead the flock or church), teachers.

Materials
Bibles, poster board, markers

Activity #3

Read and discuss the following Scriptures:

   1. Ephesians 4:16—The body grows as each part does the job it was formed to do.

   2. Philippians 4:14, 16—The Philippian church gave financially to help Paul in his missionary work. The monetary gifts were not only useful to him, but they encouraged him. When the Philippians gave him money, he knew their hearts, prayers, and support were with him. He said that the church also gained from their giving.

   3. Ephesians 6: 19, 20—Paul gained strength from other Christians who prayed for him. He asked that Christians pray for him as he preached and taught, and he asked for courage to tell people about Jesus even when he was afraid.

Now have the students write down their answers to the following questions:

   1. Identify your work in the body. (Your resource or talent.) How can you use your talents in the church and in your "world" to bring people to Christ? (*sing in church or lead in worship, write notes to encourage others, invite friends to play ball with church friends, etc.*)

   2. What are ways you can support foreign missionaries?

Materials
Bibles, paper, pens or pencils

Step 2

Have students who participated in Activity #1 share their illustrations with the class. Discuss how silly it looks if the whole body wants to be a foot or an ear wants to be an eye. God made each of us different. Look at our own bodies. Each part is different with a different function. Have students who participated in Activity #2 list all the gifts found in the Scriptures. See if the students can think of other gifts not mentioned in

Part of the Team

Scripture they could add. Now have the students who participated in Activity #3 tell ways we can support others in the body as the church supported Paul in his missionary efforts.

Step 3

Distribute photocopies of page 117 and pens or pencils. Have students write the words of service on or near the body part most likely to perform that particular service. The answers may vary, but here are some possibilities:
1. teaching—mouth, hands
2. serving—hands
3. encouraging—arms (to hug with), mouth
4. giving—hands
5. leading—legs, hands
6. singing—mouth
7. building—arms, legs
8. helping—arms, legs, hands

(Option: you could also turn the reproducible page into a transparency and have them write their words on the parts of the body that fit.)

Say to the students, "Just as we can use every part of our being to serve others, every person in the church can work together to help others also."

Materials
photocopy of page 117, pens or pencils

Take It to the Next Level

Form teams once again with the students. (They can be the original teams they started with today.) Give them these tasks:
1. Take off one shoe per person and line the shoes up in order from largest to smallest size.
2. Write down ten words that can be made out of the word *missionary*.
3. Line up and sing, "Jesus Loves Me" with the first person singing one word, the next person singing the next, and so on.

You may want to award prizes to the team that finishes the fastest.

Close the session by reminding students that we can accomplish more when we work together. Close in prayer.

Material
4" x 6" index cards, paper, pens or pencils, stop watch or timer, small prizes (optional)

We're All Part of the Body

Write the following areas of service on or near the body part that is most likely to perform them.

teaching

leading

serving

singing

encouraging

building

giving

helping

"From him the whole body, joined and held together by every supporting ligament grows and builds itself up in love, as each part does its work" (Ephesians 4:16).

Session 4

Go for the Goal!

Scriptures: Matthew 28:20; Mark 16:15; 1 Corinthians 9:22; James 1:27; 2:15, 16
Memory Verse: Mark 16:15

Know there are missionaries all over the world who need their support.
Feel a desire to assist and encourage these missionaries.
Write a letter of encouragement to one missionary.

Get Into the Game

Divide the students into two to four teams. Give each team a roll of toilet paper. Have each team write down as many ways as they can think of to be missionaries and support other missionaries in the world. Write down things the church as a whole can do to accomplish the mission, as well as what individuals can do to accomplish the mission of bringing people back to God through Christ. Write each individual idea on one square of toilet paper. Allow three to five minutes for this activity. The team with the longest list at the end of time wins. Have the team share their list with the other kids.

Material
rolls of toilet paper, fine-tipped felt pens, stop watch or timer

Step 1
Activity #1

Distribute paper and pencils. Have students number their papers from one to eighteen, then have them write a word or phrase for each of the following descriptions:

1. Proper name
2. Country
3. Noun
4. Noun
5. Verb
6. Plural Noun
7. Article of Clothing
8. Article of Clothing
9. Adjective
10. Food
11. Food
12. Language
13. Period of Time
14. Popular Saying
15. Adjective
16. Building
17. Word ending in "ing"
18. Place

When students have finished say, "Imagine yourself going across the seas to a different country such as Ethiopia. What are some of the challenges you would face?" *(a new language,*

Materials
photocopies of page 122, paper, pens or pencils

different food, weather, customs, and diseases.)

Distribute photocopies of page 122. Then say, "To give you some idea of what it might be like to walk into a totally new area and not have any idea of what is going on, let's fill this story in with the words you wrote down." Have students complete the story and then take turns reading their stories.

Activity #2

Read James 1:27 and James 2:15, 16. Say to the students, "The Bible tells us that we are to look after people who need help. We have people in this state, not too far from us, who need help. You and I don't always have the resources to help them, but others have chosen to be missionaries to these needy people in our own communities."

Instruct the students to write and produce a "good news" video tape. Have positive stories about organizations and people feeding the homeless. Have actors, live reports, etc.

Tape a local news report and see how many negative stories are reported. Use that report as the basis of your "good news" report. Take each report and write your own "good news" to replace their "bad news." For example, if they report destruction of a hurricane, then report how Christian people went in to a devastated area and supplied food and aid. If they report a robbery, then report on someone doing a good deed for another person. If they report a hate crime then report on a youth group going to a senior citizen's home to rake leaves or mow grass.

Use information concerning local benevolent missions for true stories of help in the community. Tape the news segment to play in Step 2 or have the students perform it.

Materials
video tape of an evening newscast, paper, pens or pencils, information about local benevolence missions, video camera (optional)

Activity #3

Divide students into small groups to study the material about a particular missionary. Have them answer the following questions and report to the rest of the students.

1. Who is the missionary?
2. Who is in the missionary's family? (children, spouse, ages of children)
3. What does this missionary do? (teach, preach, council)
4. What are some needs of this mission?
5. What can we do to help?

Next have each group take a popular ad slogan and rewrite it as a commercial for this missionary. For example, "We are driving excitement . . . Pontiac!" could be "We are reaching the world . . . _____ missionaries!"

Materials
information concerning missions (not used in Activity #2), paper, pens or pencils

Go for the Goal!

Step 2

Have students from Activity #1 read their mad libs. Explain that just as the mad libs seemed strange when read, moving to a foreign country would seem strange too. Ask if any of the students have ever lived in a foreign country. What were the challenges? Say, "People who live in other countries for the purpose of telling people about Jesus have these challenges too. Someday you might like to live in another country and tell people about Jesus. In what country would you like to live if you chose a foreign mission field?" Next have students respond. Have students from Activity #2 present their "Good News" live or on video. Say, "We have missionaries who live locally. They feed the homeless, take care of people with AIDS and other illnesses, and minister to kids through local sports programs for the underprivileged. They are telling people about Jesus through being salt and light in our area. If you chose one day to serve in a local mission organization, what would you like to do?"

Have students discuss. Let students from Activity #3 present their commercials for the missionaries. Ask the students what missionary they would like to visit if they had the opportunity.

Step 3

Divide the students into two teams. Give each team two sheets of paper. Send them into two separate rooms with the instruction that they are to make a house out of the two sheets of paper. After the students have been divided, give one group scissors, crayons, and tape. After a few minutes have the teams come together and present their houses. Both teams created a house, but one team had an advantage.

Say, "Missionaries in other locations have a job to do, but we can be the advantage to our missionaries. We can be like the crayons, tape, and scissors that will make their challenges easier to face. What are some things we can do?" Allow the kids to speculate. Have kids write letters of encouragement to a missionary. Take snap shots of groups and individuals to include in the letters. Have the kids commit to support one missionary for the **Bridge the Gap** and **Go to Extremes** activities (see pages 123-128).

Materials
paper, crayons, tape, scissors, note cards, pens or pencils, Polaroid camera

Take It to the Next Level

Distribute index cards and colored pencils or markers to the students. Have students write the memory verse (Mark 16:15) on the index card. Encourage students to personalize the verse

Materials
4" x 6" index card, colored pencils or markers, Bibles, gift coupons from page 127 (photocopy several for each student)

with the name of the missionary chosen for the bonus sessions.

Have the students commit to pray for this missionary every night for a week. Each time they pray for that missionary, have them draw a house on their index card. Also, have the students commit to do at least one "chore" to earn money for the missionary in the **Go to Extremes** session (see pages 125 and 126 for more details).

End this session with a prayer circle. Encourage each of the kids to say a sentence prayer asking God to give wisdom and guidance to the missionary they have chosen.

A missionary's first letter home
Mad lib

The _____ family has finally arrived in
   (proper name)
_____. Being a _____ in a
   (country)   (noun)
foreign country has been a challenge. First, we had to
raise enough _____ for support. Then we had to
                   (noun)
_____ all our _____ and
   (verb)   (plural noun)
make arrangements for the long trip. Our first challenge
was the change in weather. We had packed _____
                                                (article of clothing)
and found we only needed _____ after we got
                                 (article of clothing)
here. The food here is _____. _____ and
                             (adjective)   (food)
_____ are the main staples. The language here is
   (food)
_____. It took us _____ to learn enough
 (language)   (period of time)
just to say, "_____." Altogether things
                    (popular saying)
are going _____. We hope to build a
                       (adjective)
_____ and start _____ very
     (building)   (-ing word)
soon. We have found _____ to have
                             (place)
many challenges.

Bridge the Gap

Missions Banquet

By the end of **Session 3** the students will have been introduced to missions supported by their local congregation. They will, as a group, choose one missionary, preferably from a foreign field. The Missions Banquet will entail researching food and decorations indigenous to the area where the missionary serves. Parents and kids will work together to prepare native cuisine and room decorations. The kids will prepare games or songs that might be played or sung in that missionary field. Some possibilities include:

1. Latin American countries—serve tacos, burritos, or nachos; decorate with serapes, sombreros; play with pinatas.

2. Japan or other Asian countries—serve rice, egg rolls, chow mein noodles; decorate with fans, bonsai plants, kimonos; make origami objects.

3. Africa—serve red beans and rice, banana chips or fried bananas, pineapple, or peanuts; decorate with pictures of jungle plants and animals; play the song "Seed to Sow" by Michael W. Smith from the CD *Go West Young Man* (Reunion).

During the banquet, have someone record the students' individual messages of greeting and encouragement to send to the missionary. Have each family bring a family photo for an album sent as encouragement to the missionary.

Distribute photocopies of page 124 for families to attach their photos on and write a personal message to the missionary.

Greetings from the

[place photo here]

_____ *family!*

_____
_____
_____
_____
_____
_____
_____
_____
_____
_____
_____
_____

Toy Auction

This session can be done at the same time as the **Bridge the Gap** session or on a different date.

First, have the students commit themselves to earn money. By doing household or neighborhood chores they can earn money to bring as an offering for the missionary selected for the Missionary Banquet.

Second, ask parents to be supportive in "hiring" their children. (Involve grandparents, aunts, uncles, etc.)

Third, give the students gift coupons to be filled out for each chore done to earn money. The object is not simply to bring money to the offering, but to earn money for the offering. Make several photocopies of page 127 and cut the coupons apart for the kids.

Fourth, ask the students to bring books, puzzles, and other items that are in good condition and would be of interest to other kids their age for an auction. (You may get other church members interested in donating things that would be interesting to preteens.)

Fifth, have the students return their gift coupons and the money they have earned for the missionary. For every coupon returned, students get a credit toward the auction. No money is used during the auction, only credits. For example, with every coupon, you get $100 credit at the auction.

Select a date for the donations to be auctioned. The students use their credit to "buy" the products. This is a fun way to raise money for missions. It ends up being a book exchange with a little flair. It also emphasizes that when we give, we receive—and giving is fun!

The week before the auction, calculate the amount each child has to spend at the auction. For every coupon with offering money, a student receives $100 credit. For every offering without a coupon, the student receives $50 credit.

Give each student a number and write his name on the auction page photocopied from page 128. Use a highlighter to indicate the amount of credit they have. Put only six to ten names on a page. Once a page is full, give it to an adult. In other words, that adult needs to track children with numbers one through ten.

The auctioneer picks up an item and begins to auction in increments of $10. When the highest bidder has bid, the auctioneer says, "Sold to # ." The adult with that student's number marks the dollar amount off on the sheet. When the student has spent most of her money, the adult can tell her how much money she has left.

Continue the auction until all items are "sold."

Toy Auction Gift Coupon

_____ did a chore for
name of student

_____ for which I paid
name of person who hired student

him/her _____ . I understand this
amount that was paid

money will be used to support mission work.

Toy Auction Gift Coupon

_____ did a chore for
name of student

_____ for which I paid
name of person who hired student

him/her _____ . I understand this
amount that was paid

money will be used to support mission work.

Toy Auction Gift Coupon

_____ did a chore for
name of student

_____ for which I paid
name of person who hired student

him/her _____ . I understand this
amount that was paid

money will be used to support mission work.

Toy Auction Gift Coupon

_____ did a chore for
name of student

_____ for which I paid
name of person who hired student

him/her _____ . I understand this
amount that was paid

money will be used to support mission work.

Toy Auction

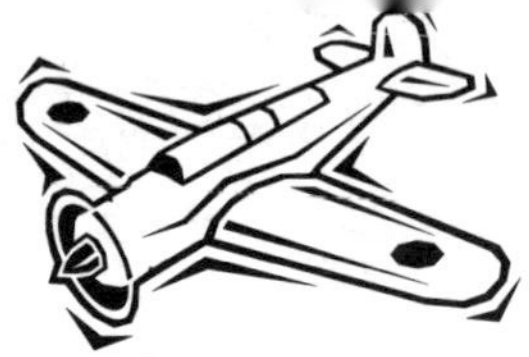

#	Name	$20	$40	$60	$80	$100	$120	$140	$160	$180	$200	$220	$240	$260	$280	$300	$320	$340	$360	$380	$400